BLACK INVENTORS

NATHAN AASENG

Facts On File, Inc.

Black Inventors

Facts On File, Inc.
11 Penn Plaza
New York NY 10001

Library of Congress Cataloging-in-Publication Data

Aaseng, Nathan.
    Black inventors / Nathan Aaseng.
      p. cm.—(American profiles)
    Includes bibliographical references and index.
    ISBN 0-8160-3407-9
    1. Afro-American inventors. 2. Inventions. 3. Technological
innovations. I. Title. II. Series: American profiles (Facts on
File, Inc.)
T39.A36 1997
609′.′273—dc21   96-40486
[B]

Text design by Cathy Rincon
Cover design by Matt Galemmo
Illustration on page 5 by Dale Williams

Printed in the United States of America

MP FOF 10 9 8 7 6 5 4

This book is printed on acid-free paper.

Contents

Introduction

Americans take pride in being a self-reliant people. We value individuals who rely on their wits and hard work to chart their destinies. We tend to scorn those who constantly rely on other people to make life easier for them.

That image of rugged individualism, however, is misleading. Few Americans can get through even a few minutes of a day without leaning heavily on the efforts of hundreds of creative geniuses. We wake up in a spring mattress bed to the sound of an alarm clock. We flick on a light switch and turn on the radio to hear weather reports compiled by satellites and computers. We take milk, pasteurized and packaged by machines and transported in air-conditioned vehicles, from a refrigerator. Our day has barely begun and already we have borrowed so many ideas and devices from others that we can hardly keep a tally of them.

We are in constant debt to inventors who created useful products and processes that we never could have devised. Yet, despite the tremendous impact of inventors on our lives, we take them for granted. Most Americans could rattle off a long list of prominent athletes or entertainment figures, yet recognize relatively few names of inventors, the people who actually change the way we live.

In compiling a list of inventors whose ideas have changed the very fabric of our lives, most people would probably cite Thomas Edison, Alexander Graham Bell, Orville and Wilbur Wright. Robert Fulton, Johannes Guttenberg, Cyrus McCormick, Samuel Morse, Henry Ford, Charles Goodyear, and Eli Whitney might appear on many rosters.

How many African Americans does the above list include? None. Most Americans would be hard-pressed to come up with the name of a single black inventor. George Washington Carver, who achieved fame for his plant research and seldom patented his discoveries, might be the lone exception. Even the National Inventors Hall of Fame, established in 1973 to recognize the work of inventors, has been slow to honor the work of an African American.

From this, one might conclude that African Americans have had little interest or success in inventing. The truth is we can hardly get through a day without taking advantage of the creative genius of black inventors. African Americans developed the processes that bring sugar to your table and shoes to your feet, that lubricate much of society's machinery, and that carry frozen pizza to your home. You cannot tee up a golf ball, bait a fish hook, or stop at a traffic signal without bumping up against an African-American innovation.

No one knows the extent to which black inventors have had an impact on our society because for many centuries there were no organized systems of documenting inventions. Good ideas were quickly imitated. With no record as to who invented what and when they did it, the true inventors were often lost to history.

In the fifteenth century, the Italians tried to bring order to the conflicting claims of inventors by establishing patents. These legal documents certifying that an individual or individuals invented a device or process are granted on the principle that the person responsible for the invention is entitled to "own" the invention, for a specified time. Others wishing to manufacture, sell, or otherwise profit from the invention must pay the inventor for the privilege of using his or her idea.

The United States government wasted little time in enacting a patent law of its own. In 1790, its second year of existence, Congress established a board for evaluating patent applications, along with a few general patent laws as guidelines. Three years later, Congress tried to simplify the system by eliminating the examination board. In order to obtain a patent, an applicant needed only to pay a fee, document the invention with descriptions and illustrations, and swear that he or she was the sole inventor of the innovation.

This honor system did not work well. Inventors complained that rivals were stealing their inventions and rushing off to the patent office to claim credit. In 1836, the federal government restored the examination system. The patent board required applicants to show that they were the first to conceive an idea, that the invention could do what the inventor described, and that it was useful and not harmful.

The government asserted that an inventor has an obligation to the society that nurtured him or her. Therefore, a patent would last for seventeen years, after which anyone in the country would have the right to use, manufacture, and sell the invention without obligation to the inventor.

Although the creation of an examination board brought order to a chaotic scramble for patent rights, it did not eliminate the barriers that prevented African Americans from gaining recognition for their inventions. Many black Americans had far less access to education and information than their white counterparts. As a result, they had no idea how to patent their inventions. Blacks also tended to have less money than whites. Patent fees were high enough to discourage even those who understood the system from applying for a patent.

Slavery further hampered inventive efforts of blacks. Most slave owners believed that educating most blacks was a waste of time and that those slaves who did learn became less willing to do the hard manual labor required of them. Some masters were so opposed to slave education that they whipped, beat, and mutilated slaves who were caught reading or learning to read. Such restrictions on learning made it difficult for slaves to develop the knowledge base and intellectual training needed to attack creative problems. Furthermore, slaves had neither the leisure time nor the equipment to carry out experiments.

Even with these handicaps, however, African-American slaves developed innovative devices and processes. The common saying that "necessity is the mother of invention" applied to most of these inventions: virtually all involved ways to save labor or improve production on the farm or in the household, where these slaves worked day after long day at their tedious tasks.

Pro-slavery advocates actually used the slaves' inventiveness as an argument in favor of slavery. According to these people, black people were lazy by nature. Only under the discipline and direction provided by their white masters, could these blacks accomplish worthwhile tasks. "When did a free Negro ever invent anything?" they scoffed.

Under patent rules passed in 1793 and 1836, slaves could legally patent their inventions. While true in theory, it was not true in practice. Masters claimed ownership of many slave inventions and obtained patents for these inventions in their own names.

This practice has made it impossible to determine how much African Americans have contributed to inventions that have reshaped our world. There is some evidence that the cotton gin that revolutionized the cotton industry was inspired by, patterned after, or even copied from a slave. Prior to developing his cotton gin, Eli Whitney took a trip to a Georgia plantation. Whitney saw that removing the seeds from freshly picked cotton was slow, painstaking work; slaves worked all day to clean seeds from just a few pounds of cotton. While touring that plantation, Whitney observed a slave named Sam using a homemade machine with a comblike device that pried the cotton fibers away from the seeds. Sam's father had invented this cotton-cleaning machine but had never applied for a patent. The cotton gin that Whitney built and patented used the same principle of comblike teeth to separate seeds.

Historians have similarly wondered about the influence of a mechanically gifted slave named Jo Anderson, who belonged to Cyrus McCormick. Many suspect that Anderson contributed to the development of the grain harvester for which McCormick became famous. But the utter disregard for the rights of slaves silenced their side of the story so that claims of African-American influence on such inventions can only be speculation.

One slave's invention came to light when his master made a public issue of asserting master's right to a slave's invention. Ned, a slave who worked on the Pike County, Mississippi plantation of Oscar J. O. Stuart, designed a cotton scraper that allowed one person working with two horses to do as much work as four people working with the conventional cotton scraper could do with four horses. In 1857, Stuart applied for a patent on the "double cotton scraper," on the grounds that "the master is the owner of the fruits of the labor of the slave, both intellectual and manual."

U.S. Commissioner of Patents Joseph Holt denied Stuart's application to patent Ned's invention, a position supported by U.S. Attorney General Jeremiah S. Black on June 10, 1858. The official reasoning was far from a victory for blacks. Holt and Black based their decision on U.S. Supreme Court rulings that slaves were not citizens and therefore could not enter into contracts of any type. This meant that slaves could neither enter a patent agreement with the government, nor assign those rights to master.

As a result of this ruling, the Confederate States of America passed a law in 1861 granting patent rights to slaves. This issue received extra attention due to the fact that Benjamin Montgomery, a slave owned by Confederate president Jefferson Davis, was a noted inventor. In the late 1850s, Montgomery invented an efficient propeller for ocean vessels. The Confederate government eventually constructed ships for their navy based on Montgomery's unpatented design. Ironically, the Confederacy, which was fighting to retain slavery, recognized the rights of slaves to their inventions, while the United States, which was fighting to end slavery did not. As a practical matter, however, there is no record of any slave obtaining a Confederate patent.

The abolition of slavery in the decade following the Civil War ended the question of slaves' rights to their inventions. That did not, however, eliminate all barriers to black inventors. African Americans continued to struggle with inferior educational and economic opportunities. The patent process remained prohibitively complex and expensive. Further, prejudice prompted many

> "A *machine invented by a slave, though it be new and useful, cannot, in the present state of law, be patented. I may add that if such a patent were issued to the master, it would not protect him in the courts against persons who might infringe on it.*"
> —Joseph Holt,
> U.S. Commissioner of Patents

blacks to disguise their involvement with their own innovations. Convinced that the value of their inventions would plummet if word got out these were the creations of blacks, African-American inventors often took out patents in the name of their white lawyers.

U.S. patent records have not required applicants to identify themselves by race. This has added to the difficulty in discovering which inventions can be credited to African Americans.

A few prominent early African Americans are known to have invented devices even though they did not patent them. Benjamin Banneker, born to a white indentured servant and a black slave in Baltimore, Maryland in 1731, was a brilliant scholar and engineer. George Washington's stepson recruited Banneker to help design the nation's capital, Washington, D.C. The project was well under way when Pierre L'Enfant, the primary architect of the new city, quarrelled with the government. L'Enfant left the country in a huff, taking all his plans with him. Banneker achieved fame by reproducing L'Enfant's entire city plan from memory so that the work continued uninterrupted. Less known is the fact that in 1754, Banneker designed and built his own clock, possibly the first ever made in the United States.

James Forten, born in Philadelphia in 1766, was a prominent early African American who, like Banneker, profited from a Quaker education. After working as an apprentice to a sailmaker, Forten enlisted in the navy during the American Revolution. His experience on the seas, combined with his knowledge of sails, helped him find a job working for a sail manufacturer.

Shortly after 1800, Forten invented a device that allowed sailors to operate and adjust sails more easily. Forten did not patent his sail control device but went into business manufacturing it, by himself. Eventually, his factory employed more than fifty workers, and profits from his sails made Forten one of the richest men in the United States.

For the most part, however, African-American inventions went unnoticed until 1894. At that time, Congressman George Washington Murray, a former slave with eight patents on farm implements to his credit, researched the patent records and read into the *Congressional Record* a list of ninety-two black inventors.

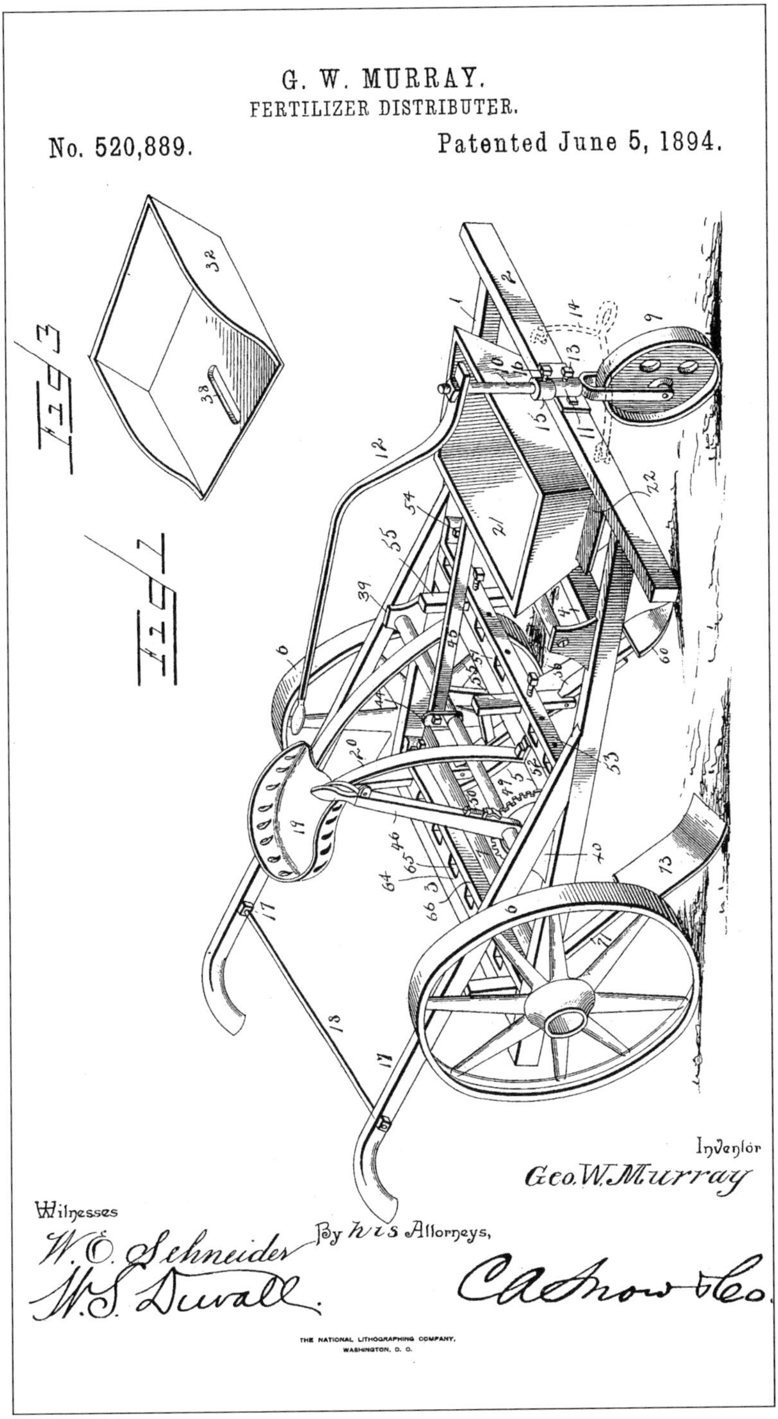

G. W. MURRAY.
FERTILIZER DISTRIBUTER.

No. 520,889.

Patented June 5, 1894.

Fig 3

Fig 1

Inventor
Geo. W. Murray

Witnesses
W. E. Schneider
W. S. Duvall

By his Attorneys,
C A Snow & Co.

The fertilizer distributor diagrammed in this patent application is one of eight patented farm implement inventions of South Carolina congressman George Washington Murray. (U.S. Patent Office)

Researchers originally credited Henry Blair with being the first African-American patent holder. Blair was an illiterate free black who lived in Glen Ross, Maryland. On October 14, 1834, he received a patent for a seed planter that allowed farm workers to plant more corn in less time with less hand labor. However, Thomas L. Jennings beat Blair by more than a decade. Jennings was born a free man in New York City in 1791. While working as a tailor, Jennings developed a process for dry cleaning clothes that he called "dry scouring." Jennings obtained a patent for the process on March 3, 1821; he used the profits from his invention to purchase family members out of slavery.

This book tells the stories of a few of the thousands of African-American inventors who followed in the footsteps of Jennings and Blair. These men and women have "perservered through the system" and changed the lives of those around them.

Many others could have been awarded a chapter of their own. George Washington Carver's work with new crops such as peanuts, sweet potatoes, pecans, and soybeans pumped hundreds of millions of dollars into the economy of the South by freeing farmers from dependence on cotton as its dominant crop. Carver, however, lived too early to have his most valuable work regarded as legitimate invention. Not until 1930 did the U.S. Patent Office approve patents for new forms of plants.

Andrew Jackson Beard was one of the few early black inventors who actually made money from patented inventions. In 1884, the thirty-five-year-old inventor sold his patent on a new type of plow for $4,000. Two years later, he patented a "Double Plow" and sold the rights for $5,200.

After a brief career in real estate, Beard went to work at a railroad yard in Alabama. There he became familiar with one of the most dangerous occupational tasks in the world—the joining or "coupling" of railroad cars. Workers hooked railroad cars together by pushing one car until its linking piece fit over the linking piece of the other car. One worker stood between the two cars to guide the linking pieces into place and inserted a metal pin that held the pieces together. The problem was that those pushing the massive car into place could not easily stop the car's momentum. Often the heavy cars

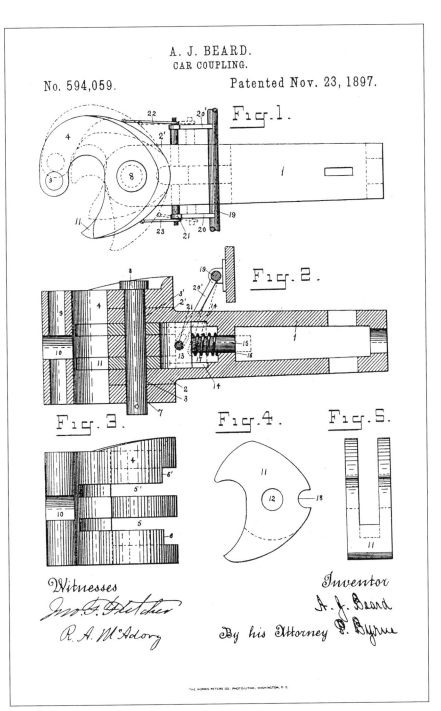

Andrew Beard's diagram of his car coupling mechanism (U.S. Patent Office)

crushed the middle man before he could drop the pin into place. Beard may have suffered a serious leg injury in this manner.

Beard eliminated the need for a worker to stand in the no-man's land between cars by creating the "Jenny Coupler," a device that automatically joined cars by simply bumping them together. He patented his coupler on November 23, 1897, and sold it to a New York law firm for $50,000—an enormous amount of money at the time.

William Hunter Diamond's case was more typical of nineteenth-century African-American inventors. Diamond, the first black graduate of the University of Pittsburgh, worked for a railroad company that operated on one of the most heavily trafficked stretches of rail in the country. In hopes of preventing accidents at busy intersections, Diamond designed a special traffic light. He used green lights to indicate it was safe to proceed, orange to advise caution, and red as a warning to stop.

After Diamond patented his device in 1906, his employer sent him to work on a project in England. Some of those familiar with the case believe that his employers kept him in England until Diamond's patent rights expired so that they could use his invention without having to pay him. Whether true or not, he reaped virtually no financial reward from his invention and died in poverty in 1956.

Otis Boykin created many useful products based on his unique electrical control systems. While working as a laboratory assistant testing automatic controls for airplanes in the 1920s, Boykin developed a special electronic resistor used in computers, radio, and television. He invented control units that operated devices as diverse as heart pacemakers to guided missiles, and also patented a chemical air filter and a burglar-proof cash register.

Dr. Meredith Gourdine provided an energy-saving boost to many industries with his electrostatic spray-painting process, patented in 1965. Gourdine's method was especially useful for painting

> "African-American patent holders should be applauded simply because they persevered through the system."
>
> —Patricia Ives Sluby, patent historian

metal consumer products such as automobiles and appliances. The owner of his own business—Energy Innovations—Gourdine has patented eighty inventions.

Emanuel Logan of Columbia, Maryland did more than simply complain about crime and safety; he used his creative genius to make the world safer. Upset over a rash of bank robberies in his neighborhood, Logan designed bullet-resistant Plexiglass, patented in 1968. After a friend disappeared from a hospital sick bed, Logan developed Door Guard, a time-delay control door latch now used by hospitals, retirement homes, theaters, airports, and government buildings to prevent confused patients from wandering and keep unwanted people out while not greatly inconveniencing authorized visitors and personnel.

Robert Shurney is an African-American inventor involved in the intricate technology of space exploration. In order to give exploration vehicles traction on the dusty, low-gravity surface of the moon, Shurney invented metal chevron wheels used in the 1970s. He also developed a waste-management system for the Skylab.

All of these people, and hundreds more, are worthy subjects for examination. This book provides only a sample of the creative work of African-American inventors who have altered the world in which we live.

A view of New Bedford, Mass. from the Fort Near Fairhaven, c. 1845. Lithograph by FitzHugh Lane after a sketch by A. Conant (Courtesy of the New Bedford Whaling Museum)

Lewis Temple

(1800–1854)

"Thar she blows!" cries the lookout atop a whaling ship prowling the North Atlantic. The ship's crew fly into action, lowering thirty-foot long boats, each with six sailors, into the ocean. The boats fan out, spraying water with their oars as they try to position themselves close to where they think the submerged whale will eventually resurface.

The whale hunters wait anxiously, bobbing up and down in the swell of the sea. Ten minutes. Fifteen. Twenty. Suddenly, the sea boils and a whale explodes through the surface, the turbulence nearly capsizing the boat. Standing at the front of the boat, legs braced to keep him from being pitched overboard, one man rears back and plunges a barbed metal harpoon deep into the whale.

The sea roils again as the wounded whale dives into the water in an attempt to escape. Hundreds of feet of rope spin out into the water from the boat as the whale plunges into the ocean depths. The crew have risked their lives getting close enough to plant the harpoon into the whale.

If the harpoon holds, the mammoth beast will eventually tire and the boats will converge and kill it.

Suddenly the rope goes slack. The thrashing and twisting of the whale has dislodged the harpoon and now the whale swims free. The risk and the effort have all gone for naught. Cursing over the loss of a whale worth more than $10,000, primarily because of its valuable oil, the crew prepares to start all over again.

In the mid-eighteenth century, an African-American inventor came to the aid of frustrated whalers. Lewis Temple devised a harpoon head that seldom came loose, no matter how hard the whale fought. The Temple Toggle Iron allowed whalers to catch more of the majestic sea creatures than ever before. The invention brought millions of dollars to the whaling industry, which wielded Temple's invention without much regard for the survival of whales.

The details of Temple's life are sketchy. Few people paid enough attention to blacks in the early nineteenth century to write down anything about their lives. Nothing is known of Temple's early years other than that he was born a slave in Richmond, Virginia in 1800.

By 1829, Temple was living as a free man in New Bedford, a city on the southern coast of Massachusetts. Biographers can only speculate how he won his freedom and came to live in New Bedford. A reasonable guess is that he escaped from the South through the Underground Railroad. More than 100,000 slaves fled to freedom through this network between 1810 and 1850. Living in northern Virginia, Temple would not have had far to go to reach the states where slavery was prohibited. New Bedford, a whaling city dominated by antislavery Quakers, provided a better welcome than most northern cities for escaped slaves.

Like most slaves, Temple received no education; he probably never learned to write his name. Despite New Bedford's tolerant Quaker tradition, racial prejudice limited an African American's choice of profession. Most white laborers refused to work alongside blacks. Even those who strongly opposed slavery often believed blacks to be inferior and capable only of menial jobs. Lewis Temple, however, was skilled with his hands and began to learn the blacksmith or metal-working trade. There was plenty of business for blacksmiths in the nearly two dozen city shops, whose main industry was outfitting the equipment for whaling ships.

Whalers had been sailing out of New Bedford for more than a century by the time Temple began work. Whales provided valuable products such as meat, bone, and oil for lamps. By the 1830s, whaling had grown to the third largest industry in Massachusetts, and New Bedford was the major whaling port.

In 1836, Temple worked in a shop on Coppin's Wharf near the whaling ships. There he fought against the prevailing disdain of blacks' abilities and established himself as a hard-working, dependable craftsman. Temple and his wife, the former Mary Clark, and their three children became well-known in the city. By 1845 he was prosperous enough to afford a new shop on Walnut Street.

Working in the heat of his glowing forge, Temple pounded out many iron tools for whalers on his anvil. Outfitting a whaling ship was an enormous task. These ships needed to start out with enough provisions for an entire voyage, which often lasted as long as two years. Some of the most important tools Temple made for these whalers were the harpoons and long lances. One New Bedford shop, similar to Temple's, produced more than 58,000 harpoons in a forty-year span.

Lances were the killing weapons. Whalers could not use them first because whales were too large and powerful to simply approach and kill. Before the whalers attempted to use the lance, the whale had to be too exhausted to fight; that was where the harpoon came in. A harpoon was a short metal spear with a barbed tip.

Throwing the harpoon was perhaps the most important task on a whaling ship, and those who could do so accurately and powerfully were highly valued. The harpoonist threw the harpoon so that it stuck deep into the whale's flesh. The back end of the harpoon was secured to over a thousand feet of strong rope attached to the ship. If the harpoon held fast, the whale could not escape, no matter how it plunged and swam. Sometimes whalers attached heavy weights to the rope so the fleeing whale worked harder and tired more easily. When the animal wore itself out, the ship could approach for an easy kill.

One of the original toggle harpoons made by Lewis Temple (The Kendall Whaling Museum, Sharon, Massachusetts)

Harpoon Types

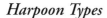

Double Barb or Double Flue

Probably the earliest type, the sharp double barbs, intended to hold the harpoon fast in the blubber or beneath the ribs, tended under great pressure to cut its way free of the flesh.

Single Barb or Single Flue

The most popular harping iron among American whalemen until the invention of the toggle iron in 1848. The razor sharp barb also occasionally cut its way free of the whale, losing it to the hunters.

Original Temple Toggle

Invented by Lewis Temple in 1848. The toggle principle was not unknown to the Eskimos. Temple's original design had a solid cast head pivoting within a split-shaft cradle.

Standard Toggle Iron

Easier to make than the Temple toggle, it was this refinement of Temple's principle that "revolutionized" the whaling industry by reducing losses. It had a solid shaft that fit into a groove in the cast head.

The Toggle-Iron Principle

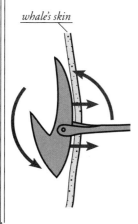

whale's skin

The "barbs," "flues," or "flukes" of the barbed irons were intended to lodge the weapon securely in the flesh of the whales, but tended to some degree to cut their way through, and thus to slip loose (though the double barb harpoon more so than the single barb iron): they simply enlarged the hole and fell out.

The importance of Temple's invention was that his harpoon could be sharpened to enter the whale as effectively as the others; but once there, a tug on the line connecting harpoon to whaleboat would swivel the head, forming a secure T. The sharp cutting edge thus turned into the whale, exposing a blunt, or rounded, surface to the skin. Hence the tearing effect was minimized and fewer whales were lost.

(Courtesy of Kendall Whaling Museum, Salem, Mass., adapted by Dale Williams)

Lewis Temple never actually took part in a whaling expedition; in fact he probably never sailed at all. But sailors loved to talk about their exploits on the high seas, and Temple heard many of these tales while taking orders and delivering his products. A recurring theme in these stories was the notorious unreliability of harpoons. Sailors would risk and sometimes lose their lives, getting close enough to connect with a harpoon only to have the whale work free with its twisting and thrashing. Sometimes the barb would slip out of the wound; sometimes the harpoon head would break off. Harpoon failure wasted countless hours of work, exposed sailors to needless risk, and cost the whaling industry millions of dollars.

Over the years, solving the harpoon problem had been a high priority among whalers. More than 100 inventors applied for U.S. patents on their harpoon improvements. As an authority on whaling wrote in 1820, "many ingenious persons had tried to improve the whaling harpoon, and although various changes had been devised, they had all given place to the simplicity of the ancient harpoon."

Temple listened to the frustration of his clients as they spoke of whale after whale that had gotten away. He figured there must be some way to design a harpoon that would not break or slip out so easily. After tinkering for awhile in his blacksmith shop, Temple found the answer. In 1848, he introduced his "toggle harpoon."

The main feature of the toggle harpoon was a moveable barbed head. This head could rotate while the shaft of the harpoon stayed still. Initially, the harpoon's head was locked into place by a short wooden pin, so that it could more easily penetrate the whale blubber. The pin was weak enough so that a slight tug would break it. This would free the toggle head so that it moved independently of the shaft and was able to adjust to the whale's twisting and jerking.

Because whalers trusted their lives and livelihoods to harpoons, they were reluctant to experiment with new models on a

> "It is safe to say that the 'Temple Toggle' was the most important single invention in the whole history of whaling."
>
> —Clifford Ashley, whaling authority

live whale. Whalers initially referred to Temple's invention as a "porpoise iron," probably because they tested it on porpoises before attempting to catch a whale.

Once whalers learned to trust it, Temple's toggle harpoon proved so effective that whalers immediately abandoned their old harpoons and switched to the new version. Now that they were able to catch and kill virtually any whale that they contacted, whalers more than doubled their catch and made enormous profits.

The more money the whalers made, the more ships they sent out in search of easy profits. During the mid-eighteenth century, more than 700 whaling ships sailed from twenty-three major ports along the New England coast. New Bedford enjoyed an economic boom, thanks largely to Temple's invention. At its peak, the New Bedford whaling industry outfitted 329 ships and employed more than 10,000 workers.

The "Toggle Iron" or "Temple's Iron," as the harpoon eventually became known, provided the basic design for the harpoons ever after. Even when whaling ships replaced hand-thrown harpoons with those shot from a gun, they continued to use Temple's toggle head.

Lewis Temple, however, benefited very little from the economic blessings he brought to the whaling industry; he never patented his toggle harpoon. As a result, almost immediately after his invention, several other New Bedford blacksmiths came out with a variation of Temple's design that could be produced in half the time for about half the cost.

Temple's invention did enhance his reputation and increase his business for a time, which led him to make plans to build a new, larger shop in 1854. However, while Temple was walking near the construction site of his new shop, he fell into a deep hole left by a city crew working on a sewer line. The blacksmith suffered injuries so severe he was unable to return to work. Temple petitioned the city, asking that it compensate him for the negligence that cost him his livelihood. The city government eventually awarded him $2,000, but Temple died a poor man in May 1854, having never received the award.

Chronology

1800	Lewis Temple born a slave in Richmond, Virginia
1820s	arrives in New Bedford, Massachusetts
1836	works as a blacksmith in a shop on Coppin's Wharf
1848	introduces his toggle harpoon
1849	other inventors create a cheaper version of his invention
1854	begins construction of a new shop
MAY 1854	dies at the age of fifty-four

Further Reading

Allen, Everett S., *Children of the Light*. Boston: Little, Brown, 1973. This book documents the whaling era in the city of New Bedford, where Temple invented his toggle harpoon.

Ashley, Clifford, *The Yankee Whalers*. Boston: Houghton-Mifflin, 1938. A classic history of the whaling industry in New England during Temple's life, includes several references to Temple.

Hayden, Robert, *Nine African-American Inventors*. Frederick, Md.: Twenty-first Century Books, 1992. This well-written collective biography includes a chapter on Temple.

Norbert Rillieux

(1806–1894)

In the late 1830s, the gold ring dangled tantalizingly just out of Norbert Rillieux's reach. He found himself trapped in the common, maddening inventor's dilemma; he had an idea that he believed was worth a fortune but could not scrape together the money to put his ambitious dream to the final test.

Whenever Rillieux came close to success, disaster would strike. He found two friends who agreed to help him perfect his sugar-purification process. Their early experiments failed due to poor equipment, however, and before they could get the proper equipment, one of the friends died.

Short of cash and help, Rillieux and Emile Barth abandoned the experiments for a time while they set about raising money through real estate ventures. The plan worked beautifully. Rillieux and Barth built up an impressive fortune, and Rillieux was about to put it to use in his experiments when the real estate market crashed in the panic of 1837. Rillieux lost virtually everything.

Rillieux pleaded with a wealthy free African American named Durnford. So convinced was Rillieux that his system would be a success that he promised Durnford $50,000 if he would allow

Norbert Rillieux (Louisiana State Museum)

Rillieux use of his sugar plant in Plaquemines Parish, Louisiana. Durnford refused. Desperate, Rillieux offered to build a sugar house at his own expense and give Durnford the fair market value of the sugar produced, if Durnford would merely supply Rillieux with the raw cane sugar he needed. Durnford turned him down.

As he headed into the 1840s, Rillieux seemed destined to be left with nothing but dreams about what might have been. Had his luck been better, had people been more open to his ideas, had he enjoyed the privileges of white society, he could have accomplished something important. Instead, he was just another of the free Negroes who were growing ever more unpopular in Louisiana.

Norbert Rillieux was born on March 17, 1806, on a plantation near New Orleans. His father, Vincent Rillieux, was a wealthy engineer—one of many Frenchmen who owned plantations near New Orleans, on land that France had recently sold to the United States in the Louisiana Purchase. Norbert's mother, Constance Vivant, originally labored for Vincent as a slave. Birth records list Norbert as freeborn. Since children inherited the legal status of their mothers, this means that Vincent must have granted Constance freedom before the boy was born.

Vincent Rillieux liked to work with machinery and devise ways to improve its performance. His most successful creation was a labor-saving, steam-operated bailing press. Vincent was pleased to discover that his son was not only extremely intelligent but had his father's curious, tinkering nature. In searching for a way to provide an education that would allow the boy to make use of his abilities, Vincent had to consider social barriers.

As child of African-American descent, Norbert could not be accepted as an equal by his father's peers. Yet Norbert's status as a free black was less unusual in New Orleans than in most of the South. While a majority of African Americans in the city were slaves, about 10 percent of the city's population was made up of free blacks, some of whom were quite wealthy and owned slaves themselves. Although white schools in the New Orleans area refused to accept any student who was not 100 percent white, the free blacks valued education highly and set up their own schools.

Vincent Rillieux decided to sidestep the racial barriers by doing what many French landowners in New Orleans did—he sent his child back to the old country for his education. His father's wealth and connections enabled Norbert to attend schools in Paris.

The shy, soft-spoken Rillieux did well in his studies. His fascination for finding ways to make machines perform tasks better and more quickly, led him to concentrate on the science of engineering. In 1930, the twenty-four-year-old Rillieux obtained a position as an instructor of applied mechanics at Paris's prestigious École Centrale. During his short teaching career at the school, he published several scientific papers on practical uses for steam.

One possibility Rillieux saw for using steam was in sugar processing, a subject that was something of an embarrassment to his French colleagues. Two decades earlier, France had invested eagerly in a new technology that extracted sugar from sugar beets. Many of the French lost heavily when their technology was unable to compete with cane sugar from the Americas. Having grown up in an area of the United States where cane sugar was the dominant industry, Rillieux had a special interest in studying sugar processing.

Common commercial sugar, which chemists call sucrose, is a product that plants create from water, carbon dioxide, and the energy of sunlight. While not essential to the human diet, most of us have become so dependent on sugar to improve the taste of food that we would have difficulty adjusting to life without it. Even if we eliminate sugar-saturated foods such as desserts and soft drinks from our diet, we still rely on sugar to sweeten the flavor of thousands of food products, from breakfast cereal to canned fruit to spaghetti sauce.

Sugar is such a common ingredient in food preparation that it is hard to imagine that it was a rare luxury in the 1830s. The sugar available on the market at that time was expensive because the process of extracting sucrose from plants was difficult and costly. Even at the high price, the finished product of the process was not the pure, smooth-flowing white granules that we take for granted, but rather an impure, sticky brown cake.

In 1830 virtually all commercial sugar came from a tall, grasslike plant known as sugar cane that grew in hot, humid climates such as that in Louisiana. Extracting sugar from the cane was a long and tedious process; long cane stalks were harvested and stripped of their leaves and then went to the sugar mill, where a press squeezed out the juice. Sugar refineries treated the juice to remove some impurities. The liquid was boiled until it thickened and formed two products:

a heavy brown syrup known as molasses, and crystals of sucrose. Centrifuges spun the mixture to separate the molasses from the raw sugar. At this point the sugar was a brown sticky mass. Refineries dissolved this material in warm water, treated it to remove more impurities, and evaporated the water to get the finished product.

The last part of the process particularly intrigued Rillieux. Sugar refineries used a crude process nicknamed the "Jamaica Train" to evaporate the water. The sugary liquid was boiled in a series of four large kettles over intense heat. Working with long-handled ladles, workers poured the boiling sugar from one kettle to another until the liquid thickened and congealed into a dark, lumpy syrup that looked like caramel. This substance was then poured into cones to dry.

The Jamaica Train was a long, hot, dangerous procedure for the workers, who sometimes suffered horrible burns. It was expensive because of the tremendous amounts of fuel required to provide fire for the continuous boiling. Furthermore, the process required a delicate touch because if the fire were too hot or the sugar boiled too little or too much, the sugar would be of poor quality.

In the 1830s, Rillieux set about to find a sugar-refining process that was safer, more efficient, easier to control, and less wasteful of energy. He immediately turned his attention to the vacuum pan, which the French had invented in 1813. A vacuum pan is a container placed in an enclosed space from which air has been removed. A vacuum was an attractive choice as a fuel saver because liquids boil at a lower temperature under a vacuum than under normal air pressure. Sugar, for example, boils at 90 degrees Celsius under 23 units of vacuum and at 70 degrees Celsius under 52 units of vacuum. Rillieux was not the first inventor to use a vacuum pan to evaporate sugar juice. Earlier efforts beginning in 1830 were "a total failure," according to author W. R. Aykroyd, that "shook for a long time the confidence of the sugar planters."

Rillieux improved upon the concept of vacuum evaporators by suggesting that steam produced by the initial evaporation step be used to heat the sugar juice in the next step. The entire "double evaporator" could be enclosed in one efficient unit.

In 1833, Edmund Forstall, a sugar manufacturer in New Orleans, learned of Rillieux's fine reputation and innovative ideas. Louisiana sugar producers were experiencing complaints from customers about the quality of their product, and Forstall hoped Rillieux could help with quality control. He persuaded him to return to the United States to assume the position as chief engineer of the Louisiana Sugar Refinery. Norbert had barely settled into his work, however, when his father had a bitter quarrel with Forstall. Out of respect for his father, Norbert immediately gave up his new job. He enlisted the aid of Emile Barth and Claudot Dumont to help him perfect his double-effect evaporator. Rillieux built and tested his first model in a sugar house run by Zenon Ranson in 1834. The test was premature because Rillieux lacked the equipment and expertise to make it work.

A series of setbacks followed that shelved Rillieux's efforts for several years. Rillieux cranked up the project again in 1841, but again his process failed to work. The inventor's prospects looked bleak in 1843, until he met another New Orleans sugar processor, Theodore Packwood. Packwood thought Rillieux's process had strong possibilities. Rejuvenated, Rillieux obtained a patent for his process and signed a contract that would pay him $13,500 for the successful installation of his evaporating system at Packwood's sugar plant in Myrtle Grove, Louisiana.

Rillieux's double-effect evaporator was an ingenious and complex piece of engineering. He recycled waste heat by placing a series of pans in such a way that he channeled the vapor from the boiling juice in the first pan into a second chamber where it heated the juice in the second pan. He increased the efficiency of the system by creating a partial vacuum to lower the boiling point of the liquids at each stage. A spout was installed so that impurities could be drawn off once they were separated from the sugar. In an energy-saving feature that was a century ahead of its time, Rillieux installed a condenser for changing the steam back to water to be recycled for use in steam-heating the first unit.

Not only was this new process efficient, it was safe and easy to operate The entire evaporation took place in an enclosed system that reduced heat and shielded workers from the boiling liquid. Nor did Rillieux's system have the problem of sugar loss from spillage that was common in the Jamaica Train. A single worker using Rillieux's method could transfer the hot liquid from one place to another simply by operating a series of valves. Rillieux further saved money for sugar processors by showing that his system could achieve good results with cast-iron kettles rather than the expensive copper kettles everyone thought necessary.

Once it was finally in place, the new process worked even better than expected. Under the old method, the hot temperatures generally caused some of the sugar to caramelize, or turn brown, instead of forming crystals; the reduced evaporation temperature made possible by the vacuum prevented this. Rillieux's factory not only cut costs dramatically but produced a purer, more crystalized sugar than other refineries.

Rillieux continued to make adjustments and improvements while supervising the Myrtle Grove plant. In 1846 he patented a more elaborate "multiple-effect" evaporator that used steam given off in the second step to heat the sugar juice in the third step. This multiple-effect evaporator was so obviously superior that other sugar manufacturers quickly adapted it. Many tried to imitate Rillieux's process, even though he was legally protected by patents. One rival took apart one of Rillieux's evaporators and tried to install it himself. He made such a mess of it, that he had to swallow his pride and call in Rillieux to finish the job.

Before long, all American sugar producers switched to the multiple-effect steam-vacuum method, providing them with a huge advantage over foreign competitors. They were able to provide high quality sugar at a fraction of the cost of such dominant sugar-producing nations as Brazil, Mexico, Cuba, and Haiti. Sugar refineries in those countries were forced to switch to the multiple-effect

"The apparatus is easily managed . . . The machine is elegant in its proportions, solid in its fixtures, and occupies a very small space in my sugar house."

—Theodore Packwood

evaporator to keep pace with their competitors. As the owner of the process patents, Rillieux became one of the wealthiest men in the state of Louisiana.

Had Rillieux been white, he could have stayed in New Orleans and enjoyed his status as one of the state's most prominent citizens. But racial tensions ran high in the Deep South in the decade preceding the Civil War. Rillieux discovered that not even wealth and a reputation as an engineering genius could protect him from social humiliation. Some of the prejudice he experienced took the form of insults, inconvenience and even segregation: the companies who employed him as a consulting engineer to modernize their facilities gave him special living quarters separate from white workers'. Rillieux was not allowed to visit any white person unless invited, and no one who was anyone in New Orleans society would invite Rillieux to his home. The professional snubs hurt even worse. Although Rillieux was one of most famous engineers in the country, scientific, technical, and engineering journals declined to mention any of his work.

With each passing year, the racial bias became more openly hostile. Southern slave owners, particularly those in Louisiana, became concerned about the increasing number of slaves who escaped from plantations with the help of northern sympathizers. Slave owners worried that runaway slaves could escape recapture by posing as free blacks. As a solution to this problem, Louisiana government officials imposed curfews and other restrictions on free blacks. In 1842, the state of Louisiana forbade free blacks from entering its borders. Any free blacks that arrived at the port of New Orleans had to stay aboard ship or risk being thrown in jail. In 1854, the law required Rillieux to carry a pass with him at all times in New Orleans. By the following year, he could not even walk the city streets alone.

Even when obeying these restrictive laws, Rillieux had no guarantee that people would leave him alone. Some people, irate that a black man could have so much wealth, threatened him with violence. The final straw for Rillieux came when he proposed an engineering plan to city government officials. During the 1850s, New Orleans was plagued by devastating health epidemics, many of which could be traced to mosquitoes breeding in swamps around the city and in the city's sewer system. Rillieux introduced a detailed engineering plan for draining the swamps and installing an updated sewer system. Despite the fact that Rillieux's plan would have saved many lives, city officials rejected it. Many of them simply refused to listen to the ideas of a black man. Years later, the city accepted and implemented a plan very similar to Rillieux's, introduced by white engineers.

Frustrated by the lack of freedom and respect, Rillieux returned to France sometime after 1855. There, he and his wife, the former Emily Cuckow, experienced less open hostility because of their race. However, Rillieux faced another frustrating barrier. He expected that his multiple-effect evaporator would enjoy the same success in Europe that it had in the United States. All he needed to do was adapt the process slightly for the sugar beet, which was enjoying a resurgence as Europe's most popular source of sugar.

Unfortunately, Rillieux's reputation as an engineer had been sullied in Europe during his years in the United States. A German engineer who worked for the Philadelphia construction company that built the first multiple-effect evaporator in New Orleans illegally copied Rillieux's plans and brought them to Europe. Based on these stolen plans, the French constructed their own version of Rillieux's evaporator at a sugar beet refinery in 1852.

As had happened with American industrial pirates, the Europeans did not understand much of what Rillieux had designed. Their evaporator was a complete failure. Instead of blaming the copiers, Europeans declared that Rillieux's invention simply did not work. Despite the massive evidence of his success in the United States, Rillieux could not overcome the damage to his reputation; few Europeans were willing to entrust their sugar beet refineries to his system.

Discouraged by a lifetime of battling prejudice and ignorance in his field of expertise, Rillieux gave up engineering. For the next ten years, he devoted his life to an entirely different field—archaeology. Rillieux immersed himself in the study and translation of ancient Egyptian writing.

For unknown reasons, Rillieux went back to work on modifying his multiple-effect evaporation system to sugar beets in 1875. Six years later, he obtained a patent for his sugar beet refining process. The French sugar industry finally converted to Rillieux's process, which caused the production of sugar to skyrocket and the cost to plunge.

Rillieux's new process brought him another influx of wealth. But again he was exasperated by the lack of respect that came with it. Although they converted to multiple-effect evaporation in the 1880s, the French stubbornly refused to admit that Rillieux's process had worked back in the 1840s.

Rillieux remained in France until his death on October 8, 1894, and was buried in his adopted country. The continued denial of his achievements bothered him until the day he died. A friend claimed, "He died more from a broken heart than the weight of years."

Rillieux's invention transformed sugar from a rare luxury used on special occasions to a household staple. By the end of the twentieth century, the average American consumed over 100 pounds of sugar per year. In addition, Rillieux's evaporation process laid the foundation for process improvements that have brought many other products, such as milk, cocoa, soap, glue, and gelatin, within the reach of ordinary people.

A general lack of recognition continues to plague Rillieux to this day. According to author Harnett T. Kane, "[Rillieux] went into the matter so long in advance of the investigations made by our modern scientists such as John Tyndall, Lord Kelvin, and others, that his success was a far more wondrous thing than can be appreciated by people of this generation."

Nearly a century after his technological breakthrough, Rillieux finally was granted the respect he so long deserved. In 1934 he received official recognition from the sugar industry for his work. The Louisiana State Museum now contains a plaque honoring one of the state's greatest inventors.

Chronology

MARCH 17, 1806	Norbert Rillieux born on Louisiana plantation
1820S	is educated in Paris schools
1830	appointed instructor at the École Centrale in Paris

1833	returns to United States to test sugar refining process
1834	builds and tests first model, not successful
1837	loses money in economic depression
1843	works for Theodore Packwood and patents his first sugar refining process
1846	patents more elaborate version of his process
1850s	leaves the United States for France because of increasing racial bias in Louisiana
1860s	studies Egyptian archaeology
1875	returns to work on beet sugar refining process
OCTOBER 8, 1894	dies at age eighty-eight

Further Reading

Aykroyd, W. R., *The Story of Sugar.* Chicago: Quadrangle, 1967. This is a detailed account of the growth of the sugar industry, and includes information on the effect of Rillieux's inventions.

Brodie, James Michael, *Created Equal: The Lives and Ideas of Black American Innovators.* New York: William Morrow, 1993. A collective biography with information on Rillieux.

Hayden, Robert, *Nine African-American Inventors.* Frederick, Md.: Twenty-first Century Books, 1992. This well-written collective biography includes a chapter on Rillieux.

Elijah McCoy

(1844–1929)

S teel wheels screeching, the fire-belching locomotive ground to a
halt. There was nothing wrong with the engine, no obstruction
on the track, no emergency among the crew. The entire train had to
stop just so Elijah McCoy could climb onto the locomotive engine
and squirt another few drops of oil into its moving parts.

Even today engine maintenance often seems a mundane, repeti-
tious task. Other than putting gasoline in the tank and air in the tires,
the oil change is the most common maintenance procedure for any
motorized transportation. For an automobile, most mechanics recommend draining the used oil and replacing it with fresh about every
3,000 miles or three months to lubricate all the moving parts and
prevent friction that can wear out parts and destroy an engine.

While modern consumers may begrudge the inconvenience of
having to make an oil change appointment or change their oil so
frequently, they would have received no sympathy from Elijah

Opposite: *Elijah McCoy.* (Henry Ford Museum and Greenfield Village)

McCoy. He had already gone through this exercise a dozen times that day and would have to do it several more times before nightfall.

"What a tedious waste of time," McCoy thought. There had to be a better way to operate an engine. In fact, there had to be more to life than this boring job, the only one he could find because no one would hire a black master mechanic and engineer. A man with his education and abilities needed more to do than shovel coal into a firebox, watch the water level in the boiler, and oil the engine every few miles.

Elijah McCoy decided to kill two birds with one stone: he would relieve his boredom by solving the problem of frequent engine lubrication. McCoy became so well-respected for producing machine-lubrication products that, according to legend, he inspired a common slang expression. Customers who ordered an automatic oil-circulating system for their machines wanted McCoy's system and not some unreliable imitation. Therefore, they often asked their suppliers if their product was "the real McCoy." The expression eventually caught on in general use until it became a catch phrase for a genuine original or high-quality article.

Elijah McCoy was born on May 2, 1844, in the Canadian city of Colchester, Ontario, near Detroit, Michigan. His parents, George and Emillia McCoy, were former slaves who had escaped from their masters in Kentucky and fled to the North with the help of the Underground Railroad. Runaway slaves lived in constant dread of slave hunters who pursued them into the northern states. Those who remained in the United States never knew when a bounty hunter might break down their door in the dead of night and drag them back to slavery. Many runaways, like the McCoys, sought refuge across the border in Canada.

The McCoys arrived in Canada with nothing but the clothes on their backs. They had no relatives or friends in the area to help them get on their feet, and they barely survived the first cold winter they had ever experienced. Elijah's father scraped out a living with odd jobs. He improved his lot by joining the Canadian army. The Canadian government rewarded him for his outstanding service in a military campaign of 1837 by granting him 160 acres of farmland. Young Elijah attended a school for black children in Colchester.

After establishing themselves in Canada for a decade, the family decided that it had nothing more to fear from slave bounty hunters, and returned to the United States. There George McCoy found work in the logging industry near the town of Ypsilanti, west of Detroit.

Elijah attended grammar school and also worked part time at a farm and in a machine shop. The boy was fascinated by machines and showed a talent for taking them apart and putting them together. His parents believed that a bright young lad like Elijah could do well in life if only he could get a decent education. They worked hard and saved all they could in order to give Elijah the education they were denied. Recognizing Elijah's special talent, and the growing role that machines played in the economy, they sought a school where Elijah could learn more about machines.

Like Vincent Rillieux, the McCoys found that educational opportunities for blacks were rare. Even people in areas of the country that opposed slavery believed blacks to be inferior and incapable of higher education. In 1860, the McCoys sent sixteen-year-old Elijah overseas to study mechanical engineering in Edinburgh, Scotland, where racial prejudice was not as strong as in the United States.

Elijah studied and worked as an apprentice in Edinburgh for five years. After earning the title of master mechanic and engineer, he stayed in Scotland for a year to gain work experience. Then Elijah returned to the United States, ready to start his career as a mechanical engineer.

Unfortunately, he discovered that the myth that blacks were less intelligent than whites dominated the business world as well as the educational system. While many companies would hire African Americans for unskilled labor, virtually none would take a chance on a black person for any skilled or management positions. Employers also hesitated to "insult" their white workers by putting blacks into positions of responsibility where they might supervise whites. McCoy applied for many jobs that required his mechanical engineering background, but failed to land any of them. To his disappointment, he could find no job more challenging than that of a fireman on the Michigan Central Railroad.

A fireman's main jobs on a train were to shovel coal into the steam engine to keep the heat up and to keep the locomotive engine parts lubricated. The only way to oil the engine was to stop the train, get out on the running board, and pour oil from cups into the engine. This was an important task because a well-lubricated machine ran better, lasted longer, and did not produce the friction that could lead to dangerous engine fires. The simple, routine tasks that any untrained person could have handled employed none of McCoy's expert training or creative abilities.

Searching for something to keep his stagnating mind occupied, McCoy started thinking about the lubricating process. Stopping a train at frequent intervals to oil the parts wasted a good deal of time. Yet no matter how often they stopped the train, the lubrication was still inadequate. The oil wore away, dripped out, or broke down quickly. This caused friction in the moving parts, resulting in heat that damaged the engine. In order to keep an engine running perfectly, firemen would have to stop the trains far more often. Trains would not be able to operate effectively if they suffered more delays than they already were.

McCoy began to wonder if there was some way to put oil into the moving parts without stopping the train. The ideal solution, he believed, would be to create an automatic device that could lubricate the engine almost continuously without the fireman being involved.

Several inventors had patented automatic lubricating devices, but none of these machines worked well. Pleased to have a project to fill up his idle time on the trains, McCoy spent many of those empty hours thinking up possible ways to create a self-lubricating machine. On his days off, he tried out his latest ideas in his tiny shop at his Ypsilanti home.

McCoy first created a system of connected channels within the engine. This would allow the oil to flow where it was needed without a mechanic poking around with an oil can into the moving parts. Oil from a single source could flow through the channels into all the areas that needed lubrication without having to stop the engine.

The more difficult problem was to find some way of making the system automatic and continuous: McCoy needed some way of providing a force that could continually push oil through the system.

This force had to be carefully controlled so that instead of flooding the machine with oil, the device would distribute just the right amount.

Gradually, McCoy developed the idea for the "lubricator cup" or "drip cup." The lubricator cup contained an oil-filled reservoir. A hollow tube extended from the bottom of the cup down into the chamber of the steam engine. Pressurized steam from the engine would rise up into the tube and activate a piston, releasing oil from the reservoir into the cylinder of the engine.

In order to regulate the flow so the steam would not blast out all the oil, McCoy fitted the top of the lubricator cup with a valve or stopcock. Once he thought of the idea, it seemed so obvious that many people could hardly believe that no one had thought of it before. One engineering expert called this stopcock the "key device in perfecting the overall lubricating system used in large industry today." With this device, machines could run continuously without shutting down for frequent oiling.

After two years of work in his shop, McCoy fine-tuned the system so that it provided a continuous drip of oil into the engine parts. He applied for a patent for his automatic lubricator that the U.S. Patent Office granted on July 23, 1872.

Unfortunately, McCoy's professional breakthrough came at a time of devastating personal tragedy. Ann Elizabeth, McCoy's wife of four years, died at the age of twenty-five, at about the time McCoy received his patent. A year later, he married Mary Elanore Delaney, with whom he spent the next fifty years.

The Michigan Central Railroad, McCoy's employer, quickly recognized the value of the automatic lubricating cup and put it to use in their trains; the invention proved to be a windfall. McCoy introduced his invention when the continual starting and stopping of machines for oiling cost companies an estimated 25 percent of their total profits. The savings with McCoy's system was even greater than that, because his continuous oiling reduced friction so much that engines and engine parts lasted far longer before they had to be replaced.

When world of the invention spread, engineers eagerly sought out McCoy. Once again, though, McCoy found that his race was a barrier

UNITED STATES PATENT OFFICE.

ELIJAH McCOY, OF YPSILANTI, MICHIGAN, ASSIGNOR TO HIMSELF AND
S. C. HAMLIN, OF SAME PLACE.

IMPROVEMENT IN LUBRICATORS FOR STEAM-ENGINES.

Specification forming part of Letters Patent No. **129,843,** dated July 23, 1872.

SPECIFICATION.

To all whom it may concern:

Be it known that I, ELIJAH McCOY, of the city of Ypsilanti, in the county of Washtenaw and State of Michigan, have invented certain new and useful Improvements in Lubricators; and I do hereby declare that the following is a full, clear, and exact description thereof, reference being had to the accompanying drawing and to the letters of reference marked thereon, which form a part of this specification.

The nature of my invention consists in the construction and arrangement of a lubricator for steam-cylinders, as will be hereinafter more fully set forth.

In order to enable others skilled in the art to which my invention appertains to make and use the same, I will now proceed to describe its construction and operation, referring to the annexed drawing, in which is represented a longitudinal section.

A represents the oil-cup, provided with the cover B. In the center of the bottom of the cup A is a downward-projecting stem, C, to be screwed into the place where the lubricator is to be used. This stem is hollow, and from the same extends a tube, D, through the center of the cup. Within this tube is a rod, a, having a valve, b, at its upper end above the tube D to close the same, and at the lower end is a piston or disk, d, within the stem C. Around the lower end of the rod a, between the piston d and a shoulder in the stem, is placed a spiral spring, e, which forces the rod down, so that the valve b will close the upper end of the tube D and prevent the passage of the oil.

When the steam presses upon the piston the valve rises and allows the oil or other lubricating material used to pass out.

In the cover B is a thumb-screw, E, directly above the valve b, by means of which the flow of oil may be readily regulated. At the bottom of the oil-cup is a faucet, G, for the purpose of drawing off the condensed steam when necessary.

Having thus fully described my invention, what I claim as new, and desire to secure by Letters Patent, is—

1. The tube D, rod a, and spring e, in combination with the valve b and thumb-screw E and top B, the several parts being arranged to operate substantially as and for the purpose specified.

2. The stem C, tube D, rod a, and piston d, in combination with the spring e, when the spring is arranged in the stem and between the piston and end of the tube, substantially as and for the purpose set forth.

In testimony that I claim the foregoing as my own I hereby affix my signature in presence of two witnesses.

ELIJAH McCOY.

Witnesses:
S. M. CUTCHEON,
W. R. SAMSON.

The brilliant simplicity of McCoy's inventions provide an extreme contrast with the mind-boggling creation of Jan Matzeliger (Chapter 5). McCoy described his lubrication

to success. McCoy received many inquiries from railroad officials eager to use his invention. When they discovered he was black, many executives withdrew their request for McCoy as a consultant and refused to buy his invention. Engineers were particularly reluctant to have a black man supervise the installation of the system. As with most inventions by blacks, they referred to it with a racial slur. McCoy's lubricator cup became the "nigger oil cup." But McCoy's

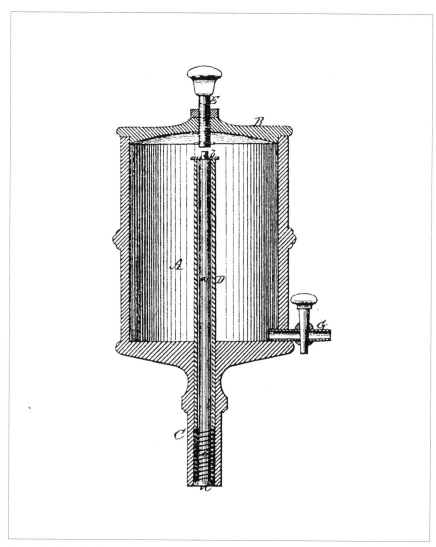

invention in a single page.   (U.S. Patent Office)

lubricator cup worked so well that virtually all engineers had to adopt it rather than commit economic suicide. From 1872 to 1915 most locomotives in the United States and many in foreign lands used McCoy's lubricator cup.

McCoy was something of a perfectionist when it came to engineering. He liked to supervise and instruct those who bought his inventions to make sure they used them correctly. Although he had solved the basic problem of the self-lubricating locomotive engine, he kept looking for ways to improve his system. Over the course of his life, he received three dozen patents pertaining to lubricating devices.

The lubricator cup freed McCoy from a life of unskilled labor. In 1882, he left the Michigan Central and moved to Detroit, where he worked full time inventing and consulting. He financed his workshop efforts by selling previous patents.

Over the years, McCoy adapted his patented lubrication techniques to work with many different kinds of engines and machines, from ocean liners to specialized factory units. McCoy introduced the basic principle of his lubricating inventions to other mechanical areas, such as air brakes. Instead of injecting oil into the system, McCoy channeled air to activate brakes.

When asked late in life what he considered to be his best invention, McCoy pointed to the graphite lubricator he patented in April 1915. McCoy developed the product in response to problems that industrialists experienced lubricating a type of engine called a superheater that ran on a tremendous amount of steam. Oil did not work well at such high temperatures. McCoy substituted a powdered substance as a lubricator. He used graphite, a form of carbon commonly used to make the lead for pencils. In powdered form, graphite is soft, greasy, and flows smoothly. McCoy created a device that could mix powdered graphite with oil or water to circulate it throughout a machine "without danger of clogging," as he proudly described it. Late in life, in 1920, he established his own business, the Elijah McCoy Manufacturing Company, in Detroit to build the components of his graphite lubricating system.

McCoy applied his creative genius to household situations as well as industrial problems. Included in his fifty-seven patented inventions were an ironing board, a lawn sprinkler, a scaffold support, a type of tire tread, a rubber heel, and a cup for administering medicine.

An 1882 version of McCoy's lubricator for locomotive cylinders (Henry Ford Museum and Greenfield Village)

McCoy's inventions became well-known for saving money and fuel, and they protected engine and machine parts. Customers looked carefully for the McCoy name on a lubricating device so they would not get stuck with an inferior product. Yet few people knew anything about the man behind that famous name.

The man behind the machines lived a quiet life with his wife, family, and a few close friends. He believed in looking out for others and took a special interest in counseling black teenage boys. Boys dropping in at a youth center in Detroit could expect to find the great inventor working as a volunteer. McCoy encouraged the boys to pursue an education and inspired them to set career goals as high as he had.

Unlike Jan Matzeliger (see pp. 47–62), McCoy took good care of himself (or was taken good care of by his wife) during his working years and seldom missed a day of work to illness. He lasted into his eighties before he experienced any health problems.

The beginning of the end came with a serious automobile accident in 1922. Mary never fully recovered from her injuries and died in 1923. Elijah, who by this time had exhausted all the money earned from his inventions, swiftly went downhill. McCoy eventually left his home to live in an infirmary for poor elderly people in Eloise, Michigan in 1928. He died the following year, leaving behind a legacy of millions of softly purring, well-lubricated engines and machines in factories, transportation corridors, and outer space.

Chronology

MAY 2, 1844	Elijah McCoy born in Colchester, Ontario
1860	travels to Edinburgh, Scotland to study mechanical engineering
1866	returns to the United States. Unable to get a mechanical engineering job, he settles for

	a fireman's position on the Michigan Central Railroad
1872	patents first automatic lubricator; first wife Ann Elizabeth dies
1873	marries Mary Delaney
1882	leaves Michigan Central and moves to Detroit to work full time as an inventor
1915	patents graphite lubricator, which he considers the best of his fifty-seven patented inventions
1923	Mary dies from injuries sustained in automobile accident. Elijah's health rapidly declines
OCTOBER 10, 1929	dies at the age of eighty-four

Further Reading

Brodie, James Michael, *Created Equal: The Lives and Ideas of Black American Innovators*. New York: William Morrow, 1993. Straightforward collective biography; contains an entry on McCoy.

Haskins, James, *Outward Dreams: Black Inventors and Their Inventions*. New York: Walker, 1991. Collective biography; contains a chapter on McCoy.

Toule, Wendy, *The Real McCoy: The Life of an African-American Inventor*. New York: Scholastic, 1993. A brief, nicely illustrated biography for young readers.

Lewis Latimer

(1848–1928)

A schoolteacher walked into the office of Crosby and Gould, a patent law firm just down the block from the school for the deaf at which he taught. Using his knowledge of how sound is transmitted, this teacher had tried for a long time to invent a device that would help the deaf to hear. Eventually he created an instrument that carried voices over wires.

Realizing he had stumbled upon a revolutionary communications tool, the teacher wanted to patent his device. He knew little about the patent system except that Crosby and Gould were experts in this area. Would they help him obtain a patent for this new communications tool?

The law firm assigned one of their best draftsman, Lewis Latimer, to the case. The teacher, however, was not the most accommodating client. His class schedule was so heavy that he could not spare any daytime hours for meeting with Latimer.

"I was obliged to stay at the office until after 9 PM when he was free from his night classes, to get my instructions from him, as to how

Opposite: *Lewis Latimer* (Schomburg Center for Research in Black Culture)

I was to make the drawings for the application for a patent upon the telephone." Latimer later recalled. Working late into the night, Latimer listened to the teacher's explanations, asked detailed questions, and put together the patent application, complete with drawings and a working model.

Neither the teacher nor Latimer was aware of how crucial Latimer's overtime would prove, but both knew that several other inventors were closing in on the concept of transmitting spoken messages over wire. Incredibly, the race to invent the telephone ended in a photo finish. Working tirelessly to complete the application, Latimer was able to deliver the finished product to the U.S. Patent Office on February 14, 1876, the same day that Elisha Gray filed a patent for an almost identical invention! Since the teacher's application reached the office four hours earlier than Gray's, he was awarded the patent for the telephone.

Had Latimer not put forth an extraordinary effort, had he kept to normal business hours or made the slightest error that would have caused the Patent Office to reject the application, the teacher, Alexander Graham Bell, would have lost not only a fortune but his place in history.

Lewis Latimer is as obscure as Bell and his contemporary, Thomas Edison, are famous. Ironically, both of those famous inventors owe at least a portion of their success to Latimer.

Lewis Howard Latimer was born in Chelsea, Massachussetts on September 4, 1848. Like Elijah McCoy (see pp. 21–31), he was the son of fugitive slaves. His father, George Latimer, was the child of a white man and a slave woman living in Norfolk, Virginia. George, who worked as a house servant when he was a boy, suffered harsh treatment at the hands of his owner, James Gray. When Gray received a jail sentence for failing to pay his debts, he sent George to jail to serve the time in his place.

As George grew older, Gray hired him out to others as a clerk, a laborer, and a stable boy. After George married another slave, Rebecca Smith, in the winter of 1842, Gray refused to allow the couple to live together and rarely permitted them to see each other. Once, when Gray caught George visiting Rebecca without authorization, he had the slave brutally whipped.

When Rebecca became pregnant, the couple could not bear the thought of their child being born into slavery, and they made plans to escape to a free state. In October of 1842, they fled into Norfolk, a port town on the Virginia coast, and hid on a ship bound for Boston. George's skin was just light enough that he could pass for white, and once the ship left the dock, the couple emerged and posed as a slaveholder and his servant. They arrived in Boston four days later.

James Gray was not about to let his slaves slip away without a fight. He posted a large reward for the slaves' capture. After discovering that the Latimers had reached Boston, he sailed there to reclaim his property.

Gray's arrival set off a whirlwind of controversy. Boston was a center of intense antislavery activity, and many of its citizens were outraged that a slave owner would dare enter their city and publicly take a black couple back to slavery. Although George was taken into custody, supporters hid Rebecca from authorities. Prominent public figures such as William Lloyd Garrison and Frederick Douglass demanded that Massachussetts protect the fugitives. One group of abolitionists founded a newsletter called *The Latimer Journal and North Star*.

Other northerners, however, were not so sympathetic; many of them agreed that Gray had a right to reclaim his property. The chief justice of the Massachussetts supreme court supported this view with a decision affirming Gray's right to take the Latimers back.

The infuriated abolitionists then surrounded the jail where George Latimer was staying. They kept a constant watch over the cell and threatened to remove the jail keeper if he handed over his prisoner. After nearly a monthlong standoff, Gray returned home with $400 raised by abolitionists to purchase the Latimers' freedom. The case inspired the Massachussetts legislature to pass the Personal Liberty Law, which prohibited state officials from helping in the capture of fugitive slaves.

Six years after the Latimers escaped, Rebecca gave birth to Lewis, the couple's fourth child. At that time, the family lived in Chelsea, just outside Boston, but they were anything but settled. They were constantly looking over their shoulders, worried about being hauled back to slavery. When the U.S. Congress passed the Fugitive Slave

Act in 1850 that allowed slave-hunters to pursue slaves anywhere in the United States and required local authorities to assist them, the Latimers moved frequently to keep a step ahead of any possible trackers.

Lewis thoroughly enjoyed school, and did so well in class that his teacher's had him skip a grade. The boy's favorite subjects were reading, creative writing, and art. When he finished his school day, Lewis often worked far into the night helping his father. George Latimer worked during the day as a barber, and earned extra money hanging wallpaper at night. Money was always tight for the family, so when Lewis reached the age of ten, he quit school to work full time for his father.

Shortly thereafter, George Latimer suddenly disappeared, never to return to his family. Some historians suspect that, because of the notoriety of his escape from the South, he lived in constant fear of violence from prejudiced whites and went into hiding to shield his family from trouble. But that does not explain why he failed to reappear after the end of the Civil War. George Latimer's reasons for leaving have never been established. All that is known is that he worked quietly as a paper-hanger in nearby Lynn, Massachussetts for forty-five years.

Their father's disappearance doomed the remaining family members to inescapable poverty. Unable to return to school, Lewis took a job selling newspapers on the streets, including Garrison's *The Liberator*, which had been so instrumental in supporting the family's flight from the South. Lewis's two older brothers went to work at a farm school west of Boston.

Even with all the children pitching in, the Latimers could not make enough money to keep ahead of the bills. Rebecca Latimer had to take employment as a stewardess on an ocean ship—a job that required her to be away from home for months, and even years, at a time. As she could no longer take care of Lewis, Rebecca sent the boy to the farm school her two other sons had attended but had since left.

Lewis was a city boy through and through. Although he remained on the farm for several years, he never got over his hatred of farm chores. One day his brother William stopped in to visit him. Seeing how miserable Lewis was, William decided to help him and a white friend run away. The boys proved just as adept as their parents at escaping from authorities. They walked, ran, hid in the fields, and stole rides on passing railroad cars. When they were famished, they went up to houses and begged for food. Eventually, the boys completed the eighty-mile trip to Boston. Lewis supported himself by working odd jobs and waiting on tables for wealthy families. His steadiest employment was as an office boy in the law firm of Isaac Hull Wright.

> "The two fortresses which are the last to yield in the human heart, are hope and pride."
>
> —Lewis Latimer

Like many former slaves and children of former slaves, the Latimers rejoiced when President Lincoln signed the Emancipation Proclamation that prohibited slavery in the rebellious southern states. Convinced that the war was a golden chance to destroy slavery in the country forever, the older Latimer brothers answered President Lincoln's call for blacks to join the United States in its civil war against the South.

Lewis desperately wanted to fight with them. As soon as he turned 16, he lied about his age so that he could join the U.S. Navy as a cabin boy. By the time Latimer's ship, the U.S.S. *Massasoit*, sailed into action, the war was already beginning to wind down. The *Massasoit* took part in some fighting along the mouth of the James River in Virginia, just a few miles from where Latimer's parents toiled as slaves. But the war ended less than a year after Latimer enlisted. After receiving an honorable discharge from the navy on July 3, 1865, Latimer returned to Boston.

With little education and no marketable skills, Latimer could find no work other than the low-level subsistence jobs he had performed all his life. The patent firm of Crosby and Gould paid him three dollars per week to work as an office assistant. The company specialized in giving legal advice to inventors and helping them apply for patents.

While performing his duties, Latimer looked over the shoulders of the company's draftsmen who prepared detailed drawings for their clients. Fascinated by their work, he took note of the books they consulted; he went out and bought copies of those books at a second-hand store, along with some other basic drawing instruction books. Over the months, he saved what he could out of his meager pay to buy used drawing instruments that he saw the draftsmen use. Latimer spent many evenings reading the books and practicing with the instruments, hoping that some day he might get the opportunity to use them.

One day Latimer arrived early for work and found a draftsman already on the job.

"Could I do some drawing for you?" he asked. The draftsman laughed, thinking that Latimer was joking; Latimer convinced him he was serious. Since no one else was in the office, the draftsman humored Latimer, giving him a minor drawing assignment. To the draftsman's astonishment, Latimer completed the task as well as any professional. After that, when his work load started to pile up, or when he was feeling generous, the draftsman gave Latimer a drawing project.

One day the head of the company saw this lowly office assistant working on an intricate drawing. He inspected the work and was amazed at its accuracy and clarity. Latimer immediately was promoted to the position of junior draftsman. Eventually, Crosby and Gould rewarded his excellence by making him the company's chief draftsman. During his eleven years at the firm, Latimer absorbed all the knowledge he could about the patent process. With his promotion came an increase in salary that allowed him to settle down to family life. On November 10, 1873, he married Mary Wilson of Fall River, Massachussetts.

While supervising the documentation of other inventions, Latimer felt the tuggings of his own creative urges. He began experimenting and drawing to see if he could invent something worth patenting. Working with a friend, W. C. Brown, Latimer developed an improved bathroom compartment for railway cars, which he patented on February 10, 1874.

Working on Bell's patent drawings was Latimer's first experience with electrical devices; he became fascinated by the possibilities. Unfortunately, he did not have the time or resources to develop his ideas. Trying to improve his situation, he left Crosby and Gould to work in the law office of Joseph Adams. But that firm did not prosper, and in little more than a year, Latimer was out of work. In 1879, he was so destitute he had to bring his family to Bridgeport, Connecticut to live with his married sister. Job prospects were so scarce that Latimer had to resort to hanging wallpaper to earn an income. Eventually, he landed a job as a mechanical draftsman at the Follansbee Machine Shop.

Latimer was working on a small drawing one day in 1880 when Hiram Maxim walked into the shop. Maxim, the founder and chief electrician for the U.S. Electric Lighting Company, was flabbergasted at the sight of a black man performing delicate technical drawings with such skill. At that time, African Americans were seldom given opportunities to learn professional skills. Maxim, who was looking to hire a quality draftsman, asked Latimer where he learned to draw. Upon discovering that Latimer learned his trade at Crosby and Gould, he hired him on the spot. Maxim had once worked for Crosby and Gould and respected their work.

The new job was a dream come true for Latimer. Electric lighting was one of the most active areas of discovery and invention at that time: just one year earlier, Thomas Edison patented an incandescent or glowing light bulb. Edison placed a small thread of carbon inside a glass bulb from which the air had been removed. Unlike metals such as copper, which conduct or allow electricity to flow through them easily, carbon resists the flow of electricity. This caused the carbon filament to get very hot. Out in the open air, the carbon would have caught fire. But in the absence of air, the element could not flame up and instead glowed, giving off light.

When Latimer began working for Maxim, light bulbs were a novelty. Since the carbon heating element, known as the filament, usually fell apart after a brief period of activity, the bulbs could not be relied upon for everyday use. But many inventors, including Maxim, saw that Edison's invention provided great possibilities for cheap lighting that was far less messy than candles and fuel lamps. Inventors raced to discover a long-lasting filament that would make electrical lighting practical for use in homes, business, and public places.

Although hired as a draftsman, Latimer got caught up in the excitement over the light bulb. He learned all he could about electricity, and how the light bulb producers formed the fragile carbon filament by burning cellulose from wood, paper, bamboo, or

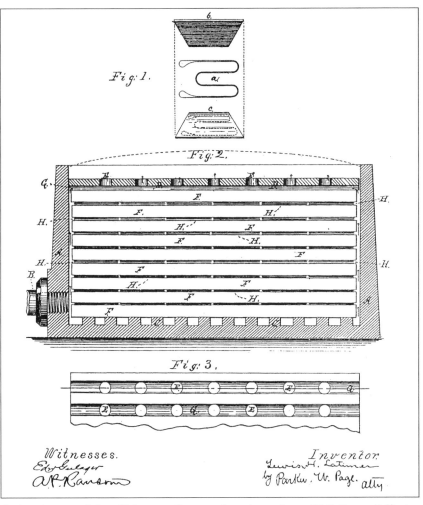

Latimer's patent design of his process for manufacturing carbons (U.S. Patent Office)

cotton to a char of pure carbon. Latimer began experimenting. After a long series of failures, Latimer enclosed a piece of cellulose in a cardboard envelope, placed the envelope in a vacuum, and gradually raised the temperature. This process produced a sturdy carbon filament that could glow for hundreds of hours. At last, light bulbs could burn brightly enough and for a long enough period of time to be practical for everyday use.

Latimer filed for a patent for his "Process for Manufacturing Carbons," on February 19, 1881. The system was so clogged by a backlog of applications for electrical inventions, that the patent was not approved until January 17, 1882. At about the same time, Latimer and Joseph Nichols shared a patent for a method of connecting the carbon filament to lead wires at the base of the lamp that improved the efficiency and durability of the lamp. Unfortunately for Latimer, the inventive work of an employee often belongs to the company: his invention became officially known as the "Maxim electric lamp."

Maxim moved his thriving operations from Bridgeport to New York City, and set up factories both in this country and abroad to manufacture the new light bulbs. Latimer went with him to New York and accepted a promotion to chief engineer of the company. During the next few years, Latimer was in great demand throughout the country. He not only took charge of the production of filaments for U.S. Electric Lighting Company in New York but also traveled around to various cities to supervise the installation of lights in buildings, rail stations, and on the streets. Latimer developed a system of parallel circuits for street lights so that if one light went out, the others would remain lit. Latimer had the joy of watching his great invention put into use to change forever the night appearance of such great cities as New York, Philadelphia, and Montreal.

Latimer took great pride in doing his work well. When requests for lamps came from French-speaking parts of Canada, Latimer undertook a crash course of French so that he could be sure his customers clearly understood all instructions. This knowledge came in handy particularly for communicating with French-speaking technicians when he set up the Montreal street light system.

In the early 1880s, Maxim sent Latimer to England to take charge of the construction of a new light factory and oversee installation of street lighting in London. While Norbert Rillieux and Elijah McCoy had both found temporary refuge from American racism in Europe, Latimer enjoyed no such luck. He was thwarted by British businessmen and workers who refused to take orders from a black man. Some British executives wrote letters to U.S. Electric Lighting, complaining that Latimer did not know what he was doing.

Latimer returned to the United States frustrated by the experience and irritated with his own boss. Hiram Maxim had been claiming credit for his employees' work. In the words of an inventor who was familiar with Maxim, "I have no hesitation in saying that in his last attempt at electric lighting he [Maxim] has made whosesale appropriation of other people's property." Despite the tremendous profit Maxim reaped from Latimer's filament process, and from further improvements that Latimer developed, Maxim never gave Latimer credit for the work. In his published autobiography, Maxim did not even mention Latimer.

Disillusioned, Latimer left the company. He spent several months working with two small companies, the Olmstead Electric Lighting Company in Brooklyn and the Acme Electric Light Company in New York, in an attempt to manufacture the "Latimer lamp" he designed. The timing was unfortunate, however, because the country had slipped into an economic depression. Both businesses failed, leaving Latimer with virtually nothing to show for his spectacular technical achievements. Now he found himself out of work at just about the time that Mary was giving birth to their first child, Emma Jeannette.

One person who recognized Latimer's ability was a fellow genius, Thomas Edison. At that time Edison was under siege from rivals who were scrambling for a share of the exploding market in electrical products. Dozens of inventors claimed to have invented electric lamps and other products before Edison, and they filed suit in court to wrestle away Edison's patent rights to those inventions. Latimer's combination of creative ability, knowledge of electricity, and experience in patent law was exactly what Edison needed to defend himself. In 1884, Edison hired Latimer as a draftsman in his company's New York City offices.

At first, Latimer worked in the Edison Electric Light Company's engineering department and then was transferred to the legal department. He frequently traveled around the country, inspecting rival patent claims and gathering information for lawsuits that attacked Edison's patent claims. He prepared technical drawings to be presented as evidence in court, and often testified as an expert witness.

Millions of dollars, as well as enormous prestige, were at stake in these patent suits; with Latimer's help, Edison won the vast majority of them. Latimer was especially effective in helping Edison battle Maxim, one of his most bitter competitors. With his intimate knowledge of Maxim's company and his personal involvement in the creation of many of its products, Latimer knew the strengths and weaknesses of Maxim's case and how best to defend Edison from Maxim's attacks. By 1892, Latimer and his coworkers had destroyed Maxim's legal assault on the Edison patents.

Latimer spent nearly thirty years working for Edison, during which time he became the company's chief draftsman and patent expert. He was a charter member (and the only person of color) of the "Edison Pioneers," an exclusive club of the company's finest electrical innovators.

Perhaps Latimer's most impressive accomplishment while employed by Edison was writing the book *Incandescent Electrical Lighting*. Published in 1890, this 140-page book was the first practical description of electrical lighting systems. Electricians considered this the definitive textbook on the subject of lighting. Since Latimer's book dealt only with Edison's system, it firmly entrenched Edison as the industry's dominant figure.

Latimer's work for Edison kept him extremely busy. Meanwhile, his eyesight deteriorated to the point where he could barely see. As a result, Latimer was not able to do much inventing on his own. Yet,

Latimer (second from right) with the staff of the Legal Department, General Electric Company, 1894 (Schomburg Center for Research in Black Culture)

in his spare time he came up with a number of creative ideas, and used his knowledge of the system to patent them. One of these was a safety elevator, which could eliminate the injuries and deaths that commonly occurred when elevators of that time misfunctioned. Another Latimer invention, intended primarily for hospitals and sick rooms, was an apparatus that cooled the air and then discharged chemicals to disinfect the air. Latimer also patented such practical inventions as a rack for hats, coats, and umbrellas, and a book support that could prevent a row of books from toppling over when one book was withdrawn from the shelf. In every case, he lacked the necessary time or finances to develop these inventions.

Far from being an emotionless, technical wizard, Latimer was a devoted family man, artist, musician, poet, and social worker. He enjoyed painting, and was especially proud of his portrait of young daughters Emma Jeannette and Louise. When he wanted to relax he took out a flute or violin and accompanied his daughters. Latimer frequently expressed himself in poetry, and upon his retirement published a volume of his poems. Throughout his life he wrote love poems to his wife:

O'er marble Venus let them rage
Who set the fashions of the age
Each to his taste, but as for me
My Venus shall be ebony.

Latimer kept active in many kinds of social causes. He worked as a volunteer to teach mechanical drawing and English to poor, jobless immigrants at the Henry Street Settlement in New York. In 1902 Latimer took charge of a petition drive to reappoint S. R. Scottron, the only black member of the Brooklyn

> "*If the electric current can be forced through a substance that is a poor conductor, it will create a degree of heat in that substance, which will be greater or less according to the quality of electricity forced through it. Upon this principle of the heating effect of the electrical current, is based the operation of the incandescent lamp.*"
>
> —Lewis Latimer

School P
Ch...

...ner also helped found the Flushing Unitarian

...'s company in 1911, Latimer worked as a
...'win Hammer, a New York City engineer
...wealthy man, he continued to work until
...'nally retired in 1924, but had no time
...', who died that same year. Four years
...he of a stroke. The Edison Pioneers
..."We hardly mourn his inevitable
...pleasant memory at having been
...or all people."

...ER 4, 1848	Lewis Howard Latimer born in Chelsea, Massachussetts
1864	joins the U.S. Navy
1865	discharged from the navy, begins work at the patent law office of Crosby and Gould
1873	marries Mary Wilson
1874	patents first invention, an improved bathroom compartment for railroad cars
1876	prepares patent for Alexander Graham Bell's telephone
1880	begins working for Hiram Maxim
1882	patents process for producing carbon filaments
1884	begins working for Thomas Edison
1892	defeats Maxim's legal challenges to Edison patents

1911	leaves Edison's company to work as a consultant
1924	retires
DECEMBER 11, 1928	dies at age eighty

Further Reading

Brodie, James Michael, *Created Equal: The Lives and Ideas of Black American Innovators.* New York: William Morrow, 1993. Straightforward collective biography contains an entry on Latimer.

Haskins, James, *Outward Dreams: Black Inventors and Their Inventions.* 1991 New York: Walker. Collective biography that contains a chapter on Latimer.

Hayden, Robert, *Nine African-American Inventors.* Frederick, Md.: Twenty-first Century Books, 1992. Another collective biography. All three cover most of the same information but add a few exclusive details.

Turner, Glennette Tilly, *Lewis Howard Latimer.* Englewood Cliffs, N.J.: Silver Burdett, 1991. One of the more detailed accounts of the African-American inventor's life.

Jan Matzeliger

(1852–1889)

When Jan Matzeliger's ship set anchor near Philadelphia, the young sailor and ship's mechanic could hardly believe what he was seeing. The shops seemed to be filled with new and fascinating types of machinery. Believing that these machines offered unlimited opportunity for a man of his mechanical ability, Jan Matzeliger boldly cut all links to the past and decided to settle in the city. Despite speaking no English, he set off in pursuit of a job. Eagerly, Matzeliger walked into a machine shop, itching to get his hands on some of this marvelous new equipment. With hand motions Matzeliger indicated that he could operate the machinery and was seeking employment. The shop owner dismissed him without a second glance.

Matzeliger entered another shop only to get the same rebuff. He tried again and again, each time more desperately, but each time the door slammed in his face without a single word of encouragement. Alone, starving, with little money and no place to stay, Matzeliger suspected he had made a terrible mistake in coming to the United States. Eventually, Matzeliger found both friends and success as an

Jan Matzeliger   (Courtesy of First Church of Christ, Lynn, Massachussetts)

inventor in this new land, but the effort would be fatally exhausting. He sacrificed most of his life in order to produce a machine that most of his contemporaries said could never be built.

☆ ☆ ☆

Jan Earnst Matzeliger was a native of the Dutch colony of Surinam (or Dutch Guiana, now Suriname) on the northeast coast of South America. He was born in Paramaribo, a small city on the Suriname River about twelve miles from the Atlantic Ocean, on September 15, 1852.

The Dutch went to great lengths to extract the economic wealth of the sweltering, wet tropical land. They imported droves of black slaves from West Africa to perform the backbreaking labor on the sugar plantations and rice fields. At one time more than 300,000 African slaves worked in Surinam under the control of fewer than 25,000 Dutch. Eventually, the slaves obtained their freedom, although the country remained a Dutch possession.

Jan's father came from a prominent, well-to-do Dutch family. The Dutch government stationed him in Surinam to supervise government machine shops in the colony. While living in Surinam, the elder Matzeliger took a black Surinamese wife who gave birth to Jan.

Jan had no memories of his mother, who died when the boy was very young. From the time he was three, he lived with an aunt. Because of his father's position, Jan grew up comfortably in the most expensive neighborhood in the city. Unlike many boys his age in Paramaribo, Jan always had a good pair of shoes, brought in to Surinam by merchant ships from New England.

Jan's race, however, prevented him from fitting in with the Dutch élite. Jan received little if any formal education. Instead, at the age of ten, he prepared for a working-class life by signing on as an apprentice at one of his father's machine shops.

Apprentices had to work long hours for many years under the guidance of experts before they mastered their crafts, but Jan enjoyed the training. He learned quickly how to use tools skillfully and showed an exceptional ability to fix broken machines.

Throughout his childhood, Jan had watched ocean vessels docking at Paramaribo to unload goods from countries thousands of miles away and pick up cargo to be sent to those same exotic ports. In 1871, curiosity about those foreign lands got the best of him. On impulse, the nineteen-year-old signed on for a two-year hitch with the Dutch East Indies Company as a crew member on a merchant ship. He broke the news to his father, who approved the plan, and to his aunt, who was stunned and upset. She would have taken the news even harder had she known that Jan would never return home.

No sooner did his steam ship sail beyond sight of the Surinam shore than the engine started coughing and spluttering. Matzeliger informed the captain that he knew something about machines and would be happy to take a look at the engine. Matzeliger got the ship running again, quickly establishing himself as one of the most valuable crew members. Whenever the ship experienced mechanical problems, the captain called for Matzeliger.

Matzeliger saw a good deal of the world during his two years at sea. He sailed around the southern tip of South America to Asia, back to the Atlantic, and up the coast of the United States. In 1873, his ship docked in Philadelphia, which was then the largest city in the United States. By this time, Matzeliger's original two-year commitment to the Dutch East Indies Company expired, and he had grown weary of life on the sea. The lure of Philadelphia's bustling machine shops was more than he could resist. Again, without a great deal of deliberation, he resigned from the ship and settled in Philadelphia. Although Matzeliger tingled with excitement when he started this new adventure in a strange city, the thrill quickly wore off. Trying to establish himself in a foreign country without any friends or knowledge of the language was miserable. Worse yet, most employers would not even consider hiring him for a skilled machinist's position because he was black.

This prejudice may have taken Matzeliger by surprise. Philadelphia was something of a haven for former black slaves, thanks to the efforts of the city's large population of antislavery Quakers. By the time Matzeliger arrived, blacks accounted for about 4 percent of the city's population, a fairly large percentage for a northern city at the time. Yet despite its tradition as the city of liberty and equality, many of Philadelphia's white residents looked down on the blacks as inferior people.

Unable to find work, Matzeliger was on the verge of starvation when he found refuge at one of Philadelphia's two dozen black congregations. The warm reception he received at a critical point in his life made a lasting impact on Matzeliger. From that point on, religion would be a focal point of his life.

For a time, Matzeliger had to subsist on menial jobs, but he never stopped trying to land a job working with machines. One day he walked into a tiny shoemaker's shop on an out-of-the-way side street. Seeing Matzeliger stare at his McKay sewing machine like a starving dog eyeing a steak, the old shoemaker gave him a trial. The new employee started out helping with odd jobs, and showed such aptitude with machines that the shoemaker let him run the McKay.

Seeing Matzeliger's growing fascination with the process, the shoemaker advised him that the best place to find skilled work in the shoemaking industry was at Lynn, Massachussetts. Lynn, a city of 35,000 near Boston, had been producing high-quality shoes for nearly 250 years; its reputation had grown until it had become the shoemaking capital of the United States, with its 170 shoe factories turning out more than half the footwear produced in the country. Good help was in such demand in Lynn that factories willingly accepted foreign workers as well as American.

In the winter of 1877, Matzeliger arrived in Lynn, not knowing a soul. As when he settled in Philadelphia four years earlier, he turned to churches for refuge. The small city of Lynn, however, did not have any black congregations. Matzeliger attended churches he hoped would be friendly, but was met with cold stares by the white members.

The tall, thin loner must have wondered if his life was nothing but a series of blunders. With the color of his skin and his poor command of English working against him, Matzeliger had a difficult time finding a job. His experience working with the McKay sole-sewing machine eventually saved him. The Harney Brothers shoe factory was in desperate need of sewers and hired him when he was able to demonstrate his skill with the McKay machine.

While working at Harney Brothers, Matzeliger began to tinker with the equipment to make it run better. He spent whatever money he could save on a set of secondhand books, *Science for Everyone*, and expensive drawing instruments with which he could draw plans for new machines. Dozens of ideas flowed from his mind. He collected patents for inventions such as an orange-wrapping machine and a railroad car coupler. Unfortunately, he was too poor to develop any of his ideas. Eventually, his employer developed and manufactured the coupler, giving Matzeliger little or nothing for it.

Matzeliger was particularly interested in developing new machines to improve the shoemaking process. Shoemaking had undergone a dramatic change in the previous thirty years due to the introduction of machines. Until that time, shoemakers had improved very little on the original methods of the Egyptians, who invented shoes 3,000 years earlier. Cobblers worked hard and long to produce one good quality pair of shoes in a day, and as a result shoes were scarce and expensive.

After Elias Howe invented the sewing machine in 1846, the shoemaking industry quickly adapted sewing machines to the production of soles and the process of putting the finished shoes together. Yet shoes continued to be so scarce and expensive that during the U.S. Civil War in the 1860s, thousands of Confederate soldiers marched hundreds of miles barefoot through mud and snow because of a shortage of shoes.

The bottleneck in the shoe industry was the "lasting" process. The last (from an Anglo-Saxon word meaning footprint) is the upper portion of the shoe that goes around the foot. Lasters shaped the leather around molds designed to fit the foot's unique contours. Both the fit and the style of the shoe depended upon the skill of the lasters. Mistakes by lasters commonly caused rips in the leather and an uneven, unattractive appearance.

Since the quality of the shoe depended so heavily on lasting, many inventors had worked diligently and spent a great deal of money trying to design a machine that could do this task automatically. The U.S. Patent Office granted eight lasting patents during the 1860s and sixty-eight the next decade. In 1872 the McKay company bought all the patents and hired inventors to use them to create a workable lasting machine. But the process was so complicated and delicate that no one had come close. There was such variation in the elasticity of the leather used for shoes that no machine could consistently produce a quality product. Most industry experts conceded that lasting would always have to be done by hand.

Lasters were well aware of their importance in the shoemaking industry. Secure in the knowledge that their jobs could never be taken over by machines, their powerful union could demand the best wages and working conditions. Lasters had no incentive to work any harder or more quickly than they desired. They sharply restricted the number of apprentices so that the few lasters in the work force became even more valuable to employers. The entire industry was at the mercy of the lasters. When lasters fell behind in their work, there was no work for other employees who depended on their often meager wages for a living. When owners balked at meeting their demands, the lasters crippled the industry by going on strike. These frequent strikes angered their fellow employees, again forced out of work because nothing could proceed without the lasters.

One day, Matzeliger grew fed up with the lasters' bullying of the industry and their boasting of their indispensability. Matzeliger began working secretly to invent a machine that could last shoes. No one had ever gotten very far with this notion, and those that made any progress at all patented their work, which meant Matzeliger had to start from scratch. He spent hours thinking about ways that a machine could perform a laster's duties. After experimenting with a variety of moving metal parts, he realized that he needed to study the hands of the lasters in action, but he could not get near the lasters without attracting their suspicions. If the lasters knew he was serious about inventing a machine to duplicate their efforts, they would not only make fun of him but would purposely block his efforts. Their influence was so strong that they could probably get him fired.

Matzeliger solved the problem by asking his boss to assign him to a new job as a millwright, whose primary duty was to maintain all the machines in the factory. Impressed by Matzeliger's skill with all types of machines, the boss gave him the position he sought. As a millwright, Matzeliger was supposed to roam the factory, checking on equipment and fixing

> "No man can build a machine that will last shoes and take away the job of the laster, unless he can make a machine that has fingers like a laster—and that is impossible."
>
> —A laster to Jan Matzeliger

machines that were not working properly. This allowed him to get near the lasters and secretly observe their actions.

Matzeliger constructed his first crude model within a year. The more he worked on the project, the more the young inventor began to believe the lasters were right. He could design one mechanical part that could imitate one hand movement of a laster, and another that could imitate another movement, but that still left dozens of other movements, all of which had to work together with great precision. How could a machine perform all the tasks of a laster on a variety of sizes, styles, and fits with different qualities of leather?

Matzeliger became obsessed with the invention. He spent almost nothing on himself so that he could devote all of his funds to the project. That meant eating corn mush every night for supper and living in a small, shabby, bare room over the West Lynn Mission in the poorest section of town. He spent virtually every available hour from Monday through Saturday working on the lasting machine. Shivering in the unheated apartment during the freezing winter, Matzeliger sketched designs and built models with parts cut from old cigar boxes and scraps of wood, wire, and nails. One design after another failed.

In the fall of 1880, Matzeliger produced a primitive cigar box model of a lasting machine. This model did not come close to performing the job of a laster, but it provided the basic design for how such a machine might be built.

The secret of his project slipped out before he was ready. People curious about his work knocked on his door. Most of those who looked at the model saw only its simple, toylike form. They laughed at it and remained all the more firmly convinced that a lasting machine was impossible.

One observer, however, saw the possibilities. An inventor who had tried and failed to design a lasting machine offered Matzeliger $50 for his model. Matzeliger was caught in a bind. Fifty dollars was a lot of money to a desperately poor inventor. Matzeliger had reached the point where he could go no further with his invention without the funds to get better materials; he could never make a working machine with parts made from material scraped together from trashbins. The offer seemed the only way he could get the money he needed to complete his dream.

Yet Matzeliger hated to give away the result of so much sweat and sacrifice to someone who could use that model as a guide for beating Matzeliger to the working invention. After agonizing over the dilemma, Matzeliger decided to sell, then changed his mind at the last instant. Somehow, he would find a way to get the materials and tools that he needed.

Matzeliger rooted through junkyards and factory wastebins for larger and stronger pieces of metal. He saved scraps from broken machines and machine parts at the factory. But these raw materials were useless unless he could find a machine or tools of his own with which to shape them. Since Harney Brothers had no forge with which he could create gears and other components, Matzeliger looked elsewhere for work. He took a job with the Beals company, whose factory had not only a forge but an old lathe that the inventor could use for precision-shaping the metal. Furthermore, this employer provided Matzeliger with a small space in the factory in which he could do his inventing.

For two more years, Matzeliger worked his regular job during the day and spent most of his evening hours on his invention. In his most difficult moments, he drew strength and comfort from his most prized possession. Before he had left Paramaribo, his aunt had given him a jar of green nutmegs and coffee beans preserved in alcohol. Matzeliger could look at it and remember that far away, someone who loved him was hoping and praying for his success.

The shy inventor also finally found a social outlet, thanks to Enna Jordan, a buttonholer at the shoe factory. Jordan saw that the quiet young machinist had no friends. She invited him to join Christian Endeavor, a young adult group from North Congregational Church that got together for parties, recreational activities such as skating, and Bible study. Matzeliger so appreciated the welcome and encouragement he received from Christian Endeavor that he attended church services regularly and even taught Sunday School.

Matzeliger edged closer to completing his task. He produced a rickety model that could perform all the tasks of a laster. But the clattering old lathe quickly fell apart. Desperate for funds, the

J. E. MATZELIGER.
LASTING MACHINE.

No. 274,207.   Patented Mar. 20, 1883.

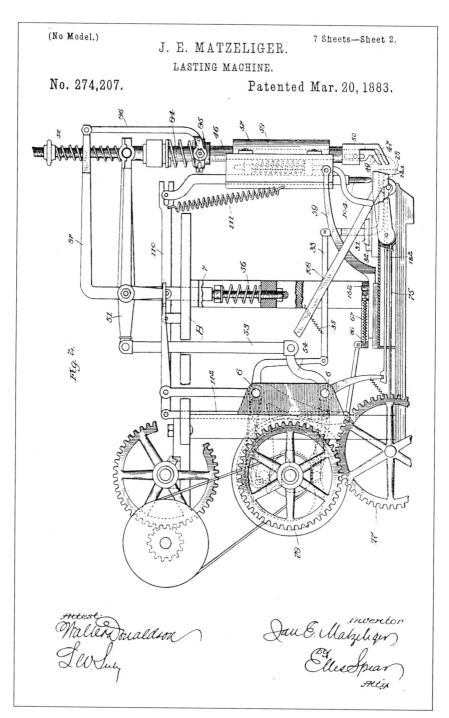

The incredible complexity of Matzeliger's design baffled patent officials. These are just two

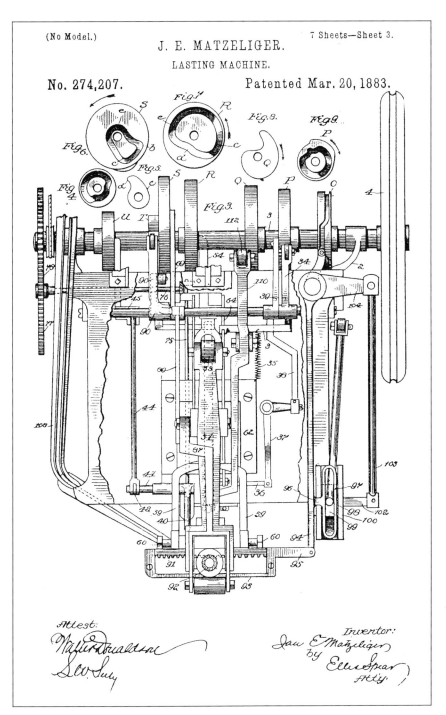

of seven drawings Matzeliger included in his patent application.   (U.S. Patent Office)

JAN MATZELIGER

inventor crammed his day further, taking a part-time job driving a horse-drawn coach. Working himself to exhaustion, he became increasingly frustrated as he realized that even with his superhuman effort he would never be able to afford the quality materials he needed to finish the job.

A fellow inventor then dangled a powerful temptation in front of Matzeliger. He offered Jan $1,500 for the rights to only the part of his machine that turned the leather around the toe. All Matzeliger had to do was sign the agreement, and he could escape his miserable lifestyle. But he could not bear to give up even a part of what he had made, even for a fortune. The fact that someone offered him so much money for a small piece of his machine convinced him he was very close to completing his dream. He turned down the offer and clung to the hope that somehow he could see his invention completed.

Finally, though, Matzeliger had to face the fact that he could never finish his machine and patent it on his own. He spent what few minutes of free time he could muster pounding on the doors of prominent Lynn businessmen, looking for someone willing to finance his dream. Door after door shut on Matzeliger. Investors had heard many proposals from inventors who claimed that they could create an automatic lasting machine. One investor reportedly lost $100,000 in a failed attempt to produce such a machine. Most businesspeople laughed at the idea that a black man could succeed where so many had failed.

Finally, two wealthy local investors, Charles H. Delnow and Melville S. Nichols, took the time to look closely at the model Matzeliger invented. Impressed by what they saw, they offered to provide all the funds that Matzeliger needed to finish his invention in exchange for two-thirds ownership of the invention. Matzeliger realized it was the best offer he could hope for, and accepted.

In late 1882, the inventor completed his lasting machine and applied for a patent. His machine was so complex that it required seven pages of detailed drawings and eight pages of descriptions. Patent officials could neither understand the diagrams in the application, nor believe the machine actually worked. A patent official traveled from Washington, D.C. to get a firsthand look at what the inventor was claiming. Matzeliger performed a demonstration in which his machine gripped, fitted, and nailed in place a shoe in one minute. That demonstration earned him a patent, received on March 23, 1883.

Even then, the machine could not quite perform up to the standards of the hand lasters for all models of shoes. Nor could it hold up to the hard use required in a factory. Matzeliger worked for two more years to improve the quality of his patented invention. On March 29, 1885, he was ready for the final test. As Matzeliger watched in triumph, his machine turned out seventy-five pairs of women's shoes, each perfectly formed.

Although the lasters and a few other detractors ridiculed the invention as the "Nigger Head Machine," most industry experts immediately recognized its worth. Neither Matzeliger nor his investors felt confident that they could build and run a business on the scale required to meet the overwhelming demand for lasting machines; they joined another firm to form the Consolidated Hand Lasting Machine Company, controlled by wealthy businessmen Sidney Winslow and George Brown. Before long the company employed 250 workers at its Beverly, Massachussetts plant, racing feverishly to keep up with orders.

The lasting machine revolutionized the shoe industry. Overnight, it broke the power of the lasters to dictate the terms of production. An experienced hand laster, working steadily for ten hours, could produce a maximum of fifty pairs of shoes in a day. With Matzeliger's machine capable of turning out from 150 to 700 quality shoes per day, hand lasters were no longer necessary. By 1899 nearly 3,000 lasting machines were turning out 80 million shoes a year in United States factories. According to industry analyst Ross Thomson, "It is a tribute to Matzeliger's accomplishment that his machine took practical form for some shoes in a decade whereas [other systems] required a quarter century."

The greatest impact of the machine was on consumers. The hand lasting machine not only dramatically increased the number of shoes produced but also slashed production costs. Shoemakers were able to pass these savings along to the customers. As a result, by 1890, shoes were plentiful and easily affordable.

The story did not end as happily for Matzeliger as for the consumers he served. Although everyone in the shoe business was well aware of the inventor's accomplishment, Matzeliger remained an industry secret. Most customers enjoyed the benefits of cheaper, high quality shoes without ever hearing of the person who made them possible.

Matzeliger sold the remaining rights to his patent to Winslow and Brown in exchange for stock in the company. With his great quest completed, he looked forward to a more normal, relaxed life. Finally, he would have time to enjoy such interests as oil painting (he was skilled enough to have taught classes in painting). He could spend more time with his few friends, and perhaps even settle down with a family.

But in October of 1886, only a year after his machines began pumping out shoes, he came down with what appeared to be a cold. The congestion got worse and Matzeliger grew so weak and tired that those close to him became alarmed. His friends the Durgins took the inventor out of his small, unheated room above the mission and brought him to their house where they could care for him.

Few were surprised to discover that Matzeliger had contracted tuberculosis. The disease struck so often in the shoe industry that the people of Lynn referred to it as the shoemakers' disease. The many years of sleepless nights, missed meals, exhausting toil, and neglect of his health had made Matzeliger a prime candidate for the illness.

Matzeliger's condition gradually worsened until a doctor ordered him to the hospital. He died there on August 24, 1889, at the age of thirty-seven. The modest, pleasant young man had given his life to the pursuit of a dream. He never had time to enjoy the fruits of his labor. But he took steps to see that the people who befriended him during his lonely existence would reap the rewards he earned. In his will, he left some of his valuable company stock to his friends, the hospital, and the doctor who cared for him. He provided a scholarship for a Christian Endeavor member to attend college and a seminary for religious training. Most of the stock, however, went to North Congregational Church. The only residue of bitterness in Matzeliger's life was the stipulation that the church could not use the money for any person or project connected with the Lynn churches that snubbed him when he first came to town. Matzeliger's final gift to this world was to allow a financially struggling church to pay its debts and continue its mission.

Chronology

SEPTEMBER 15, 1852	Jan Earnst Matzeliger born in Paramaribo, Surinam
1862	works as apprentice in father's machine shop
1871	sets sail as a crew member of Dutch East Indies Company merchant ship
1873	settles in Philadelphia, despite knowing no one in the United States and having no knowledge of English
1877	moves to Lynn, Massachussetts in hopes of finding a better job working with shoe manufacturing equipment
1880	finishes first cigar box model of shoe laster
1883	awarded patent on automatic lasting machine

1885	successfully completes test that demonstrates his machine is ready for the production line
1886	develops tuberculosis
AUGUST 24, 1889	dies at age thirty-seven

Further Reading

Mitchell, Barbara, *Shoes for Everyone.* Minneapolis: Carolrhoda, 1986. This slim biography of Matzeliger's life for younger readers contains some fictionalization, necessitated by fact that little information exists on Matzeliger's life.

Thomson, Ross, *The Path to Mechanization: Shoe Production in the United States.* Chapel Hill, N.C.: University of North Carolina Press, 1989. This scholarly work provides details and statistics on the industry during Matzeliger's time, as well as information about Matzeliger's contributions.

Haskins, Jim, *Outward Dreams: Black Inventors and Their Inventions.* New York: Walker, 1991. A collective biography that contains a chapter on Matzeliger.

Granville Woods

(1856–1910)

On the evening of January 13, 1882, the Atlantic Express, carrying 260 passengers, chugged along the banks of the Hudson River toward New York City. The train was twenty-three minutes behind schedule, which put it only about fourteen minutes ahead of the Tarrytown Special, headed in the same direction on the same track.

As the Atlantic Express veered east toward the Harlem Bridge, its brakes mysteriously activated. The train squealed to a halt in the middle of the track, where it sat while engineers tried to figure out what had gone wrong. It was still there fourteen minutes later when the Tarrytown Special roared around the bend and smashed into the stalled train. The rear cars crumpled under the impact and burst into flames. Eight passengers, including State Senator Webster Wagner, burned to death in the inferno.

While this was one of the more notorious examples, such train collisions were all too common in the 1880s. The *New York Times* lists dozens of entries under "train wrecks" for each six-month period of the decade. The glut of trains running on the tracks to service the

Granville Woods (Schomburg Center for Research in Black Culture)

growing demands of customers, and the lack of communication between those trains, made passenger travel by rail a risky venture.

The long litany of train tragedy caught the attention of Granville Woods. Although he lived a life of obscurity, Woods was well-known among the many rivals competing for dominance in the new field of electronics in the late nineteenth century. He was such a gifted inventor that some referred to him as "The Black

Edison." By the end of the 1880s, Woods developed a sophisticated and reliable telegraph system that helped make the modern railroad possible.

Ironically, Woods had to fight both Edison, the man to whom he was compared, and the other great African-American electrical inventor, Lewis Latimer, in order to retain the patent rights to this life-saving invention. Refusing to be intimidated by Edison's prestige and legal clout, Woods met the Edison Company's challenge in court. Latimer seldom lost a court battle while working for Edison, but met his match in Woods. Unlike most inventors, Woods beat the giant of the American electrical industry, not only once, but twice.

Granville T. Woods was born on April 23, 1856, in Columbus, Ohio. Virtually nothing is recorded about his parents or his childhood. The area in which he grew up originally had been a stronghold of antislavery sentiment. The Northwest Ordinance of 1787 had outlawed slavery in what eventually became Ohio, but that did not mean blacks were welcome. The state of Ohio passed laws in the early 1800s prohibiting blacks from entering the state unless they posted a bond of $500. Since few blacks could afford this sum, the law effectively sealed off the border from African-American migrants. That raises the strong possibility that the Woods family lived in Ohio since before the laws were passed.

Granville Woods may have been among the first black children in his area to attend school. The decades-old Ohio law banning black children from attending public schools was modified shortly before Woods reached school age.

Woods attended elementary school until the age of ten, when he dropped out because his family needed the money he earned. Although he received no more formal education for the next ten years, he was an observant, curious lad. No matter what situation Woods found himself in, he absorbed all the information he could and then made use of that knowledge to move on to a better position.

When he took on a job in a machine shop that repaired railroad equipment, Woods became fascinated by machines and read whatever he could find about them. With money saved from his wages, he paid a master mechanic at the shop to give him private instructions on how to work the equipment.

In 1872, the sixteen-year-old Woods went west in search of adventure. Like many young black men wandering off into the world, he found that life's harsh realities took much of the fun out of the adventure. Woods needed to work to support himself, and yet no one would hire him. Fighting off discouragement, he eventually landed a job with the Iron Mountain Railroad in Missouri. Woods proved such an able worker that he moved up to positions of more responsibility. Like Elijah McCoy, he worked as a fireman on the train. Like McCoy, he spent his spare moments on the job reading and experimenting with equipment.

Two years later, Woods settled in Springfield, Illinois where he found work at a mill that rolled iron and steel into plates and bars. He grew restless, however, with the routine duties, so in 1876, he indulged his love of learning by attending school. Biographers are not certain where he attended and identify the school only as "an eastern college," probably a technical school. Woods spent two years taking evening classes in electrical and mechanical engineering while working six and a half days a week at a machine shop to pay for his education.

Upon completing his studies, Woods signed up as an engineer on the British steamship *Ironsides*. During his two-year hitch, the *Ironsides* sailed to ports all over the world. With his thirst for adventure satisfied, Woods returned to Ohio in 1880. He hoped that his wide experience with engines and machinery would qualify him for challenging work. Like fellow mechanical wizard Elijah McCoy, he found no employers willing to entrust a position of high responsibility to a black man.

Woods was employed by the D & S Railroad in Cincinnati and worked on a steam locomotive. After four years of going nowhere in that job, Woods conceded that he would never get the kind of challenge he craved if he continued to work for others. In 1884, he and his brother Lyates formed the Woods Electric Company.

When he started his business, Woods found innovative solutions to the problems that faced him. He had not been in business a year before he earned a patent on a steam boiler furnace.

In 1885, Woods patented an invention that combined two of the most important inventions of the century. Forty-seven years after Samuel Morse invented the telegraph and nine years after Bell invented his telephone, Woods produced his own device that combined telegraph and telephone technology to transmit electrical messages with greater range than previously possible. Woods called the concept "telegraphony," and sold the technology to the Bell Telephone Company. Both Granville and Lyates were bitten so badly by the inventing bug that they quickly sold both their patent rights and their electric company to devote all of their time to inventing.

Woods's experiments with electric transmission of messages brought to his attention the problem of train safety. During the 1800s, train traffic had become heavier and heavier, especially in the urban areas along the East Coast. Several trains had to use the same track during the day, and any delays or problems could create a disaster. Trains pulled such heavy weights that even after they applied their brakes they could not stop for hundreds of yards. Without some method of early warning that other trains were approaching on a collision course, engineers risked their lives each time they set out on a trip.

With the invention of the telegraph, railroad officials thought they had a way to solve the problem. They tried placing one telegraph operator on each train and another at the station. The operators aboard the trains signaled their positions to the station operator, who alerted other trains in the vicinity.

The railroad operators divided the railways into sections to create a "block" system. A train was not supposed to leave one block section and

"*There is no inventor of the colored race whose creative genius has covered quite so wide a field as that of Granville T. Woods.*"

—Henry Baker, assistant examiner at the U.S. Patent Office

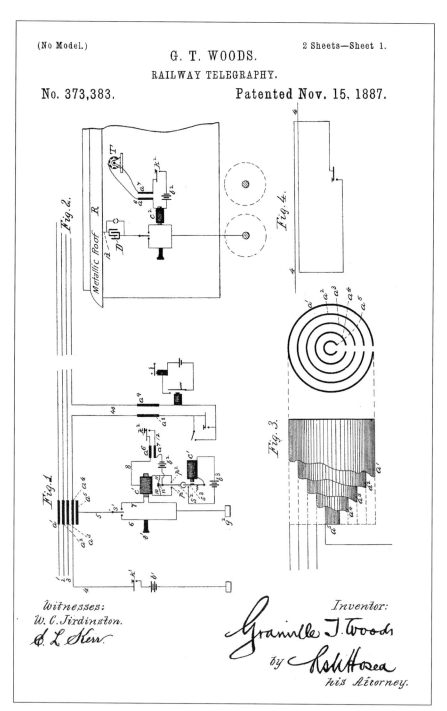

G. T. WOODS.

RAILWAY TELEGRAPHY.

No. 373,383.

Patented Nov. 15, 1887.

Witnesses:
W. C. Jirdinston.
S. L. Kerr.

Inventor:
Granville T. Woods
by Roh Hosea
his Attorney.

Diagram included in Woods's application for railway telegraphy patent (U.S. Patent Office)

enter another until it received clearance from the main station. But miscommunications and poor connections persisted, causing serious accidents. Sometimes the messages did not get relayed quickly enough, or the relayed message was inaccurate. The station operator could not always receive and interpret all the incoming messages correctly. The most serious problem was keeping a moving train's telegraph wire connected to the station's telegraph wire. Electrical engineers tried running telegraph wire through all the train tracks and having each train equipped with an electrical connection that was supposed to stay in contact with the telegraph wire. Unfortunately, the bumping and jostling frequently broke the contact and interrupted communication. Somehow, the railroads had to come up with a more reliable method of maintaining contact between trains and stations. Many inventors tried to come up with ways to solve these problems.

Granville Woods thought the answer involved using the principle of electrical induction. Induction is the ability to use a strong electrical current flowing through one conductor to produce a flow of electrons in a neighboring electrical conductor.

As with other attempts at linking trains through telegraph, Woods's system laid a primary wire in the tracks. This was connected to a battery, a telegraph key, and a sounder at the station. Each train was equipped with its own telegraph equipment, which was connected to an electrical cable suspended from the beneath the car. As the train traveled along the track, this wire remained eight to ten inches above the wire laid in the ground. If the current in the ground wire was strong enough, it could transfer current to the train. In that way, each train could send signals to, and receive them from, other trains along the track.

In 1885 Woods tried out his "Synchronous Multiplex Railway Telegraph" on a section of the New Haven Railroad in New Rochelle, New York. It worked so well that he applied for a patent, which he obtained in 1887.

Building upon his knowledge of electrical currents and trains, Woods then constructed an ingenious miniature electric train at the Coney Island amusement park in 1892. The train was unique because it ran without using exposed wires or secondary batteries. Woods placed a block of iron between the rails every twelve feet along the

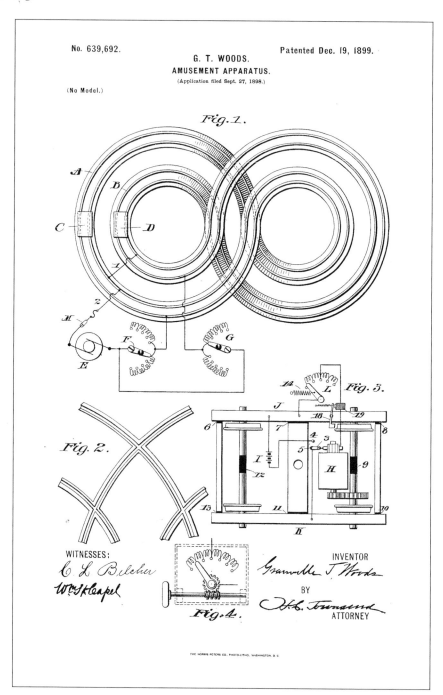

Woods's patented amusement park electrical ride thrilled patrons of the Coney Island amusement park in New York. (U.S. Patent Office)

track. Using an intricate system of magnets and switches, he sent electrical current to each block to recharge the train as it passed over them.

One of the greatest barriers to the use of practical electrical machines was the difficulty of varying the speed of rotating shafts and other mechanical parts. Machine operators found that many tasks could be accomplished with precision only if they could vary the speed of the mechanical parts with which they worked at the touch of a button.

The problem was that in electric machinery, the speed at which mechanical parts moved was controlled by the amount of electrical current. Changing the amount of electrical current coming into the machine was totally impractical. It would involve the time-consuming job of altering the voltage supply at the source.

The only known way to change the speed of a rotating shaft *without* changing the voltage at the source was to install a large resistor in the machine that could drain off some of the current coming into the machine. Unfortunately, this was like reducing the flow of gasoline into an engine by spraying most of it out the exhaust. The resistors not only wasted a tremendous amount of electricity, but quickly became scorching hot, which damaged the machines. Woods solved the problem by inventing a device called a dynamotor, which regulated motor speed with much smaller resistors that reduced the heat and the electrical waste. *Cosmopolitan* magazine called this dynomotor Woods's "most remarkable invention."

As with many inventors in the fiercely competitive electronics world, Woods had to defend himself against other inventors claiming his ideas. On two occasions he sued the giant Edison Company for making use of his patent ideas without paying for them. The Edison Company argued in court that they were the originators of the Woods's inventions. One of these cases involved a system similar to Woods's Synchronous Multiplex Railway Telegraph. Woods defended himself well and proved in both cases that he was the first applicant and that he used no other model source for his work. Thomas Edison was so impressed by Woods that he adopted an "if you can't beat them, join them" philosophy. He tried hard to recruit

Woods, offering him prestigious positions with the company. Woods preferred to be his own boss and declined all offers.

During his career, Granville Woods collected more than fifty patents, almost all dealing with electricity. He invented an automatic air brake, a new method of tunnel construction, an automatic cutoff that improved the safety of electrical circuits, and improvements in the telegraph, telephone, and phonograph. He obtained a patent for an electric egg incubator, the forerunner of modern machines that can hatch 50,000 eggs at a time.

Although Granville Woods never became a household name, his reputation as an electronics genius spread throughout the industry. Major companies such as Westinghouse, General Electric, and American Engineering purchased rights to his ideas.

Little is known of Woods's personal life other than that he moved from Cincinnati to New York City in 1890 and remained there until his death. Supported by his brother, he churned out invention after invention. But like so many African-American inventors, Woods was unable to translate his creative achievements into wealth. For most of his life, Woods barely had enough money to survive from day to day. He died a poor man on January 30, 1910, in New York City.

Chronology

| APRIL 23, 1856 | Granville T. Woods born in Columbus, Ohio |
| 1866 | drops out of school at age ten to work |

1872	leaves home, seeks work on his own
1876	attends college, probably on the East Coast
1878	obtains work aboard the *Ironsides*
1880	returns to Ohio, begins working for the D & S Railway Company
1884	with brother Lyates forms Woods Electric
1885	patents telegraphony system; tests synchronous multiplex railway telegraph
1887	patents synchronous multiplex railway telegraph
1890	moves to New York with Lyates
1892	invents electric train for Coney Island
JANUARY 30, 1910	dies at age fifty-three

Further Reading

Brodie, James Michael, *Created Equal: The Lives and Ideas of Black American Innovators.* New York: William Morrow, 1993. Straightforward collective biography contains a chapter on Woods.

Haskins, James, *Outward Dreams: Black Inventors and Their Inventions.* New York: Walker, 1991. Collective biograph;: contains a chapter on Woods.

Hayden, Robert, *Nine African-American Inventors.* Frederick, Md.: Twenty-first Century Books, 1992. Another well-written collective biography. All three cover most of the same information but add a few exclusive details.

Ives, Patricia Carter, *Creativity & Inventors.* District of Columbia: privately published, 1987. Woods's life is poorly documented. This personal project done by a patent worker contains a bit more information than most on Woods.

Sarah Breedlove McWilliams Walker

(1867–1919)

Sarah McWilliams pulled a comb through her hair and then looked anxiously at the teeth; she groaned with despair at the clumps of thick, black hair she found. Yet another hair-loss remedy had failed!

The hair loss McWilliams was experiencing was a common problem for young African-American women around the turn of the twentieth century. Poor diet, illness, and damage to hair from popular hair-straightening treatments, such as tightly tying string around sections of hair, all contributed to the problem.

Severe stress only aggravated the problem, and McWilliams had more than her share of that. She worked fourteen-hour days scrubbing clothes in her washtub, trying to support herself and her daughter, Lelia, and somehow save enough money to provide Lelia with the education she never had.

Opposite: *Sarah Breedlove Walker* (Indiana Historical Society, negative #C2140)

McWilliams tried every hair-loss remedy on the market, but none of the highly touted "miracle" cures worked. She tried dozens of home remedies, often formulated her own treatments in her washtub, and then tested them. Yet the hair on her scalp continued to thin.

Despondent over her appearance, McWilliams begged God for help. As she later told the story, aid came suddenly in a dream. "A big black man appeared to me and told me what to mix for my hair," she recalled. She had to send to Africa for some of the ingredients required for the treatment, but when she tried the mystical remedy, it worked like a charm. "In a few weeks, my hair was coming in faster than it had ever fallen out."

This inspiration launched one of the most incredible business careers in American history. The poor laundress developed a line of hair-care products that transformed her into Madam C. J. Walker, the first self-made woman millionaire in the country.

The success story of Sarah Walker is all the more remarkable because, as formidable as the barriers were that thwarted African-American men's efforts at inventing, they were mere speed bumps compared to the obstacles that African-American women faced. In addition to slavery, absence of legal rights of ownership, lack of or inferior education, and poverty, which they shared with black men, black women labored under sex discrimination.

For many decades, American society viewed technical and mechanical skills as purely the domain of men. Even many who viewed blacks as uneducable acknowledged that a black male slave could tinker with some piece of machinery to make it run better. After all, that was "men's work." Women were confined to domestic chores such as cooking and cleaning.

Legally, women remained second-class citizens until the twentieth century. Even after the Fourteenth Amendment recognized the rights of blacks as voting citizens, women could not vote and had few legal rights.

The combined result was that women were strongly discouraged from any kind of inventing, and the few that overcame these obstacles

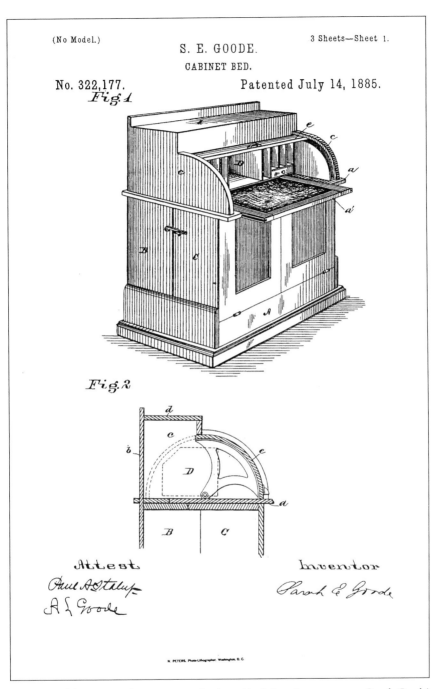

Diagram of first patented invention credited to a black American woman—Sarah Goode's cabinet bed (U.S. Patent Office)

SARAH BREEDLOVE MCWILLIAMS WALKER

had trouble getting legal rights to their creation. Through the eighteenth century, men commonly obtained patents in their own name for their wives' inventions; not until 1809 did the U.S. Patent Office award a patent to a woman.

The first African-American female listed in U.S. Patent Office records was Sarah Goode, the owner of a furniture store in Chicago. In 1885, Goode patented a "Folding Cabinet Bed," similar to today's hide-a-beds.

A prime example of a skilled black woman inventor unable to overcome social barriers was Ellen Elgin of Washington, D.C. A pioneer member of the Woman's National Industrial League, Elgin spent years perfecting a clothes-wringing apparatus in the 1880s. She never took out a patent on her invention, however, and instead sold it for $18 to a person interested in manufacturing the product. Her device proved to be a successful money-maker for the buyer. When asked why she sold her invention so cheaply, Elgin replied, "If it was known that a Negro woman patented the invention, white ladies would not buy the wringer."

The woman most responsible for changing that situation was born to Owen and Minerva Breedlove on December 23, 1867. Sarah Breedlove was the first of the family's three children to be born free. The Breedloves had worked as slaves on the Burney cotton plantation in Louisiana just across the river from Vicksburg, Mississippi prior to gaining their freedom at the end of the U.S. Civil War in 1865. Poor and uneducated, they had little choice but to stay on the plantation and work as sharecroppers—farmers who worked the land in exchange for a pitifully small part of the profits. Like her older brother and sister, Sarah had to work in the fields by the time she was six; she could attend school only when there was no crop to tend.

Throughout her childhood, tragedy compounded hardship. Sarah's parents both died of yellow fever when she was seven. For a few years, Sarah stayed on the farm with her older sister Louvenia, barely surviving by doing laundry. In 1878, another yellow fever epidemic swept through the Mississippi Delta, killing more than 3,000 people. When the cotton crop also failed, the sisters found few neighbors had the money to send out their laundry. They moved to Vicksburg hoping to find work.

Louvenia married a man who was mean and abusive to Sarah. Desperate to escape his cruelty, Sarah married Moses McWilliams at the age of fourteen. A daughter, Lelia, was born to the couple in 1885. But two years later, Moses was killed in an accident. That left Sarah, now twenty years old, uneducated and unskilled, without anyone to help her support and raise her two-year-old daughter.

The South, with its discriminatory laws, open racism, and white supremacist organizations, was a hostile environment for blacks. Like many African Americans at that time, Sarah decided to leave the South and try her luck in the North. She moved up the Mississippi River to St. Louis, where she heard there were jobs for laundresses. Sarah worked long days washing clothes and delivering clean laundry. While Lelia attended the city's public schools, the illiterate Sarah tried to make up for her lost education by attending night school.

It was during these years that Sarah's hair started falling out. In her quest for a hair grower, she tried a product made by the Poro Company. Founded by African American Annie Turnbull Malone in Lovejoy, Illinois in 1900, the Poro Company was the first significant hair product company to target black women. Malone sold products such as Wonderful Hair Grower as well as a hot comb she patented in 1900. Upon moving to St. Louis in 1902, the company built up its business by advertising in the black newspapers.

Sarah McWilliams worked for several weeks as a sales agent for Poro, but was not satisfied with their products. After her dream revealed the formula that solved her problem (apparently sulfur was the key ingredient, although Sarah never publicly revealed the secret), Sarah began sharing her preparation with friends. She realized that most hair-product companies designed their products for whites, and that black women were crying out for products more suited to them. Now struggling to finance Lelia's private-school education at the all-black Knoxville College in Tennessee, Sarah saw a chance to escape the low-paying drudgery of the laundry tub. Despite the misgivings of friends who thought she had lost touch with reality, Sarah decided to go into business on her own, selling to friends, acquaintances, and neighbors. Efforts to expand, however, faced stiff, sometimes hostile, competition from the established Poro Company. Annie Malone accused Sarah of imitating her products and selling them as her own, an accusation that was inevitable given the similar names of some of the rivals' products.

In 1905, Sarah received word that a brother in Denver had died, leaving behind a wife and young daughters. With Lelia away at college, Sarah saw this as an opportunity to help out the family and at the same time get a fresh start free from conflict with Poro. On July 21, 1905, the thirty-seven-year-old laundress arrived in Denver with less than two dollars to her name.

Sarah established herself by taking a job as a cook and selling her products part time. Her primary products were her hair grower and a steel hot comb with widely spaced teeth, specially designed for African Americans' thick hair. Acting on the advice of a St. Louis friend named Charles Joseph "C. J." Walker, a newspaperman with some experience in mail order advertising, she placed ads in black newspapers.

The business began to take off when Walker came out to Denver to marry her on January 4, 1906. The two set up a full-fledged business under the flashy name of "Madam C.J. Walker Manufacturing Company." C. J. helped his wife expand her advertising to black newspapers throughout the nation. An advertisement showing Sarah's hair before and after treatment was especially effective.

The enterprise seemed a success, but Sarah and C. J. had conflicting views of where success would take them. C. J. was content to maintain a small business with modest profits. Sarah was willing to risk all their earnings on the more adventurous dream of a nationwide company. The split in business and lifestyle philosophy widened throughout their marriage. The two soon went their separate ways, and were divorced in 1912. Nevertheless, Sarah kept the alluring name of Madam C. J. Walker, and C. J. continued to work as a sales agent for the company.

Part of Sarah's dream was to create a lucrative business run by women, to inspire and empower women to go beyond the routine, low-paying work that society reserved for them. In 1906 she brought Lelia, fresh from college, to Denver to manage the company while she set out with missionary zeal to win new converts to her products.

Walker's efforts to increase business were handicapped by a lack of access to the usual outlets for her products. The department stores and pharmacies that normally sold hair-care products were owned by whites who had no interest in stocking their shelves with new products for African Americans. Walker turned instead to black institutions such as black women's clubs and churches. She sought out and made friends with influential black leaders.

A relentless promoter, Walker traveled thousands of miles throughout the United States, the West Indies, and Central America, spreading the word about her company. Nearly six feet tall and flamboyantly dressed, Madam C. J. Walker attracted attention wherever she went. Despite her lack of education, she was a spellbinding speaker. She believed passionately that black women needed to pay more attention to their appearance in order to gain the respect of whites that they needed to succeed in a white-run world. Walker was selling not just products but a philosophy and a system of hair care. "I want the great masses of people to take a greater pride in their appearance and to give their hair proper attention."

Walker's most remarkable talent was her business sense, developed without any training. Pioneering a concept later used successfully by Mary Kay Cosmetics and others, Walker recruited and trained thousands of black women as sales agents. In 1908, Walker started Lelia College in Pittsburgh, Pennsylvania, to teach recruits the Walker system of health care. Dressed in white blouses and long black skirts, Walker's trained agents went door-to-door throughout the country, selling an ever-expanding line of hair-care products and cosmetics tailored to the needs of African-American women. To bolster morale she formed the Madam C. J. Walker Hair Culturist Union of America and held annual conventions at which women could meet to share encouragement.

By 1910, Walker claimed more than 1,000 field agents. Almost all were poor black women who had previously been locked in exhausting, low-skill, low-paying jobs. Sarah Walker beamed every

In her dress and her choice of transportation, Madam C. J. Walker shows the flair that made her a nationally known figure. (Indiana Historical Society, negative #C2225)

time she heard from a sales agent who thanked her for providing a decent work opportunity that pulled her out of a life of despair.

Among Walker's many travel destinations was Indianapolis, Indiana. The city's facilities and central transportation location so impressed her that in 1910 she moved her headquarters to the city. For the most part, she kept to her goal of having women in charge of the operations. Alice Kelly, for example, worked for many years as the Indianapolis factory foreperson. An exception was the hiring of Freeman Ranson. Walker met Ranson on a train where the young man was working as a porter to support himself at the Columbia School of Law; Ranson eventually took over the administration of the company.

By 1912, Walker's company was one of the most profitable black-owned businesses in the country. Yet she continued to face prejudice, not only from whites, but from African-American men. The 1912 Negro Business League Convention in Chicago totally ignored her astounding success story. When a friend politely asked that she be allowed to speak from the floor of the convention, league president Booker T. Washington ignored her. Walker sat around for three days listening to less accomplished businessmen tell their stories. Finally, after listening to a Texas banker drone on, she could take it no longer. As Booker T. Washington rose to thank the speaker, Walker came forward and demanded recognition. "Surely, you are not going to shut the door in my face!" she challenged. Her impromptu speech was soon the talk of the convention. Washington and the league were so impressed that they invited her to be the main speaker at their 1913 convention in Philadelphia. "The girls and women of our race must not be afraid to take hold at business endeavors," she told the Philadelphia gathering.

Walker's company generated controversy among blacks over the sensitive issue of African-American beauty standards. Some ministers railed against her from the pulpit, attacking her for trying to change the way God made black women. Others accused her of feeding myths of black inferiority by encouraging black women to look like whites, particularly with her hair-straightening formulas. Walker answered her critics by saying that she merely encouraged black women to take pride in their appearance. "Let me correct the erroneous impression held by some that I claim to straighten hair," she said. "I deplore such an impression because I have always held myself out as a hair culturist. I grow hair."

Walker's tireless promotion and astute business strategy enlarged the company into a multimillion-dollar business. In fact, by 1917, the Madam C. J. Walker Manufacturing Company was the largest black-owned business in the United States.

> "I *am a woman who came from the cotton fields of the South. I was promoted from there to the washtub . . . and from there I promoted myself into the business of manufacturing hair goods and preparations . . . I have built my factory on my own ground."*
> —Sarah Breedlove Walker

Walker was not shy about spending her earnings. In 1917 she had a twenty-room mansion, the Villa Lewaro, built in Irvington, New York, along the Hudson River. With her usual emphasis on empowering African-American businesses, she commissioned a black architect to design the mansion. She intended the estate, including such striking items as a gilded piano, as an inspiration to African Americans to let them know that they could achieve things they previously had not thought possible.

Walker used a great deal of her money to support educational opportunities for blacks. She donated $100,000 to found a girls' academy in West Africa, paid the salary of a teacher at a black prep school, and generously supported Negro colleges and homes for orphans and for the elderly. She also expressed her thanks to the city of Indianapolis by her support of the city's YMCA.

The frenetic pace of travel and promotion began to catch up with Walker in 1918. Her blood pressure soared so high that doctors ordered her to slow down. She tried to retire and live a more peaceful life at Villa Lewaro, but found herself incapable of relaxing. She could not free her mind from business and other civic involvements: before long she was back on the road.

During a trip to St. Louis in 1919 to promote a new line of products, Walker collapsed and had to be rushed home by a private railroad car. The first American woman to earn $1 million died of kidney failure due to high blood pressure on May 25, 1919.

Black activist Mary McLeod Bethune paid tribute to Walker by saying, "She was the clearest demonstration I know of Negro woman's ability recorded in history." The legacy of Madam C. J. Walker continues. The building she constructed in Indianapolis has been converted to the Madam Walker Urban Life Center. The company that she founded still operates out of that city and holds a share of a black hair-care market that has grown to a $2 billion per year industry. In the meantime, black American women have broken the old barriers to patent devices ranging from a hot air duct heating system to a compressed air torpedo discharger to a three-dimensional illusion transmitter.

Chronology

DECEMBER 23, 1867	Sarah Breedlove born on Louisiana cotton plantation
1874	both parents die in a yellow fever epidemic
1878	another yellow fever epidemic forces Sarah and her sister to move to Vicksburg, Mississippi
1881	marries Moses McWilliams
1885	daughter Lelia is born
1887	Moses dies in an accident; Sarah eventually moves to St. Louis
1902	Poro Company moves to St. Louis. Their products fail to cure Sarah's hair loss. Sarah begins experimentation, aided by dream
1905	moves to Denver; begins selling her products
1906	marries C. J. Walker; names her company Madam C.J. Walker Manufacturing Company
1908	founds a training school for the "Walker" beauty method in Pittsburgh.
1910	moves operations to Indianapolis; boasts more than 1,000 sales agents
1913	addresses Negro Business League Convention
1917	builds Villa Lewaro in upstate New York
MAY 15, 1919	dies at age fifty-two

SARAH BREEDLOVE MCWILLIAMS WALKER

Further Reading

Bundles, A'Lelia Perry, *Madam C. J. Walker*. New York: Chelsea House, 1991. Very detailed and complete account of Walker's life, this book dispels inaccuracies and distortions in other accounts.

Hayden, Robert C., *Nine African-American Inventors*. Frederick, Md.: Twenty-first Century Books, 1992. This collective biography contains an interesting overview of African American women inventors.

Haskins, Jim, *One More River to Cross*. New York: Scholastic, 1992. This collective biography of inspirational African-American lives includes a chapter on Walker.

Garrett Morgan

(1877–1963)

A cluster of curious onlookers gathered at a New Orleans fairground as a man piled an evil-smelling concoction inside a tent. Beside him, a dark-skinned man began putting on a loose suit and a helmet to which a pair of hoses were attached.

"Ladies and gentlemen!" shouted the white man. "Here to demonstrate my spectacular new invention is Big Chief Mason, a full-blooded Indian from the Walpole reservation in Canada! Inside that tent we have placed tar, sulfur, formaldehyde, and manure. Yes, we have even added to that a quantity of lethal ammonia gas. Imagine the noxious fumes that these materials would give off if we were to set fire to them! "Believe it or not, that is exactly what we are going to do. Before your very eyes, Big Chief Mason will stand in that tent, trapped in the thickest of the lethal smoke. Let's see what happens when the chief stands amid the fumes wearing my patented Morgan Helmet."

He set the materials ablaze until, as a New Orleans reporter wrote the next day, "The smoke was thick enough to strangle an elephant."

Garrett Morgan (Western Reserve Historical Society, Cleveland, Ohio)

The assistant, wearing the odd-looking suit, strode into the tent and closed the flap. Spectators in the front rows gasped and coughed from the smoke that leaked from the tent.

The Indian remained in the tent. Five minutes passed. Ten minutes. The crowd twittered and murmured, wondering how the Indian could possibly still be alive. Fifteen minutes passed. Twenty. Finally, the flap opened and Big Chief Mason strode out, removed his helmet, and smiled at the crowd, as fresh and healthy as when he had entered the poisonous room.

This exhibition was one of many that the white inventor and his Indian assistant performed to demonstrate the effectiveness of the Morgan Helmet, commonly called a gas mask today. The audience never imagined that they were witnessing a staged act. For while the fire and noxious fumes were real, the performers were not. The white man posing as the inventor was actually a friend of the inventor. The invention was the brainchild of "Big Chief Mason," not an Indian but an African American named Garrett Morgan! Morgan found people so hostile to a product introduced by a black person that he had to resort to the impersonation to sell his product.

Garrett Augustus Morgan was born on March 4, 1877, in Claysville, Kentucky, a small town just north of Lexington. His mother, Elizabeth Reed Morgan, had been born a slave. She and Garrett's father, Sydney Morgan, struggled to support their large family on earnings from their small farm.

Garrett was the seventh of eleven children in the Morgan family. Typical of many children in that rural community, he attended school only through grade five and then sought work. Since there was little work for him around Claysville, he left home at the age of fourteen. Like many job-seekers in the area, he headed north for the nearest large city, Cincinnati, Ohio, where employment was rumored to be more plentiful.

Like the other inventors in this book, Morgan found many people willing to hire a black laborer. He had a talent for fixing broken items, and so he worked for four years as a handyman, doing odd jobs and repairs for wealthy white people. Associating with highly educated people made Morgan aware of his unpolished background and minimal education. Believing that he needed to present a more refined appearance to get a better job, he used his earnings to hire a tutor to help him with his grammar.

In 1895, Morgan moved to Cleveland with barely a cent to his name, hoping to find a job working with machinery. He slept in boxcars while he tried to scrape together some money sweeping floors in a factory. Eventually, Morgan found a job as a sewing machine adjuster for Roots and McBride, a clothing manufacturer. Morgan enjoyed the challenge of repairing broken machines and fine-tuning them to perform precision work. He became so good at it that over the next decade he found steady work fixing and adjusting sewing machines for several companies.

Realizing his skills were in high demand, Morgan decided to go into business for himself. In 1907 he began repairing and selling sewing machines from his own shop. His business had begun to prosper by the time he married Mary Ann Hasek, with whom he was to have three sons, in 1908. The following year, Morgan made use of his knowledge of sewing machines to expand his business into a tailoring shop that produced coats, suits, and dresses. Before long, Morgan's busy shop employed thirty-two workers.

Morgan was always seeking ways to get more out of his equipment. He patented his first invention, a sewing machine improvement, and sold it for fifty dollars. A far more profitable discovery came to him while he was working on a simple problem that plagued all clothing manufacturers. The faster the sewing machine needles bobbed in and out of the material, the more friction they built up. In a short amount of time the needles became so hot that they scorched the fabrics, particularly wool. Clothing manufacturers applied various kinds of polish to the needles to reduce the friction.

Morgan was experimenting at home with a new formula for an improved needle polish when Mary called him to supper. Searching for something handy to wipe the liquid polish off his hands, Garrett grabbed a pony-fur cloth on his work bench. When he returned to work after supper, he noticed that the wiry strands of pony hair were straight.

At that time, straight hair was fashionable; curly hair was not. Morgan recognized that a product that easily straightened curly hair would be popular. He asked to borrow his neighbor's Airedale, a wire-haired breed of dog. When he applied the substance to a section of the dog's hair, the hair straightened. Morgan then took a chance and applied the liquid to his own hair. Pleased with the result, Morgan put his new product into a cream and formed the G.A. Morgan Hair Refining Company. He eventually developed a hair dye and a curved-tooth iron comb, which he added to his line of products.

> "The object of the invention is to provide a portable attachment which will enable a fireman to enter a house filled with thick, suffocating gases and smoke."
>
> —Garrett Morgan

As with his clothing business, Morgan's new company prospered. He earned enough money that he could afford to buy his own house and send for his mother to come live with him. Morgan was the first African American in Cleveland to buy an automobile.

With his businesses producing the necessary income, Morgan could afford to experiment with a variety of inventions. As the owner of a business that combined machines and a large number of people in a single enclosed space, Morgan was concerned about the possibility of deadly fires. The danger hit home when he read news reports of the terrible Triangle Shirtwaist Company fire in 1911 in New York City. One hundred forty-six workers had been trapped and killed in the factory. The thick, deadly smoke thwarted firefighters' efforts to get at the victims.

Shortly after the fire, Morgan designed a helmet that could help a firefighter survive smoke and deadly fumes. His "gas inhalator" consisted of a durable hood that fit over the head and two long tubes that ran from the hood to the floor. One tube was for taking in air. Morgan placed the opening of the tube, lined with absorbent material, at floor level below the smoke, which tends to rise. When the absorbent material was moistened just prior to use, it cooled the incoming air and prevented smoke and dust particles from being pulled in with the air. The second tube was for exhaling.

Morgan later improved the helmet so that it used a bag of compressed air, which prevented any possible contamination of the wearer's air supply. Morgan equipped his device with enough air to last for about 20 minutes. In talking with firefighters about what they wanted in a rescue helmet, he learned that they were concerned about how quickly they could put on and take off his device. Morgan redesigned the hood so that a firefighter could be fully equipped in seven seconds and could remove the hood in three seconds.

On his patent application, Morgan called his invention a "Breathing Device." When he set up another company to manufacture and sell his invention, he used the brand name "Morgan Helmet." Over the years, customers called the device by many names, including gas inhalator and gas mask. By any name, the Morgan helmet was an instant success.

Morgan did not even wait for patent approval before taking his device to the market. Ever the astute businessman, Morgan recognized that the best way to sell his invention was to demonstrate it. He especially targeted the firefighters who could most benefit from the "Morgan Helmet."

On September 15, 1914, the fire chief of Yonkers, New York tested the Morgan helmet against a leading competitor's product. Volunteers entered the smoke-filled tent that became the cornerstone of Morgan's sales pitch, equipped with one of the two hoods. While the firefighter in the rival hood staggered out after fourteen minutes, the one wearing the Morgan hood emerged after twenty-five minutes showing no ill-effects. Fire chief J. T.

"What is the use of fighting fires all night when you can do the work in fifteen minutes? Two men with a Morgan Smoke Hood and a good fire extinguisher can do more in the first 15 minutes than a whole company can do in the next half hour."

—J. T. Martz, Akron, Ohio fire chief

Martz of Akron, Ohio was so impressed by the Morgan helmet, he recommended his firefighters have one readily available at all times. Morgan's invention passed every test that fighters created for it and won First Grand Prize at an international safety and sanitation exposition in New York.

With such solid approval, Morgan expected to sell a great number of Morgan helmets, for which he obtained a patent on October 4, 1914. Many fire departments, however, canceled their orders after learning that Morgan was black. Further, when he traveled around the country, amazing audiences with his dramatic tent demonstrations, Morgan ran into the problem of racial prejudice. He discovered that sales dropped off dramatically when he presented himself as the inventor. Morgan had to hire a white "front man" to do the sales pitches, while he posed as a Canadian Indian assistant.

On July 24, 1916, a catastrophe catapulted Morgan's hood into the public spotlight. Late in the evening, a crew from the Cleveland Waterworks was hard at work expanding the 16,000-foot-long Tunnel Number Five underneath Lake Erie as part of its effort to provide water for city residents. Unfortunately, they tapped into a well of natural gas. An explosion rocked the tunnel with such force that it tore up small tracks and twisted conduit pipes.

At 9:30 P.M., William Dolan, who was stationed at the entrance to the tunnel, heard a dull boom. The earth shook as a blast of wind roared out of the tunnel and threw him against a door. Just before he passed out from the poisonous fumes that wafted up from the tunnel, Dolan managed to shut a safety door and sound the alarm.

Plant officials determined that the explosion had trapped nearly three dozen workers in a pocket of deadly gas 282 feet below the surface of Lake Erie. Immediately, plant superintendent John Johnson and six other volunteers descended into Tunnel Number five. The narrow, low passages were so saturated with smoke, dust, and deadly gas that the rescuers collapsed in fits of coughing and gagging as they neared the bottom of the tunnel shaft. Seeing the men begin to weave and fall, William Dolan rushed down to save them. He pulled Johnson and one other man to safety before collapsing himself.

Two hours later, another plant superintendent, Gustav Van Duzen, headed a second team of volunteers that braved the poisonous fumes to rescue the trapped men. Only four of the eleven workers in this rescue party staggered back to safety. They managed to haul out

Morgan posing with an early version of his smoke hood (Western Reserve Historical Society, Cleveland, Ohio)

one of the fallen members of the first rescue party but reached none of the original trapped workers. The rescuers were beside themselves with fury and frustration over the lack of safety equipment that would have enabled them to save the trapped tunnelers.

Over the years, Morgan's role in the events that followed grew into a legend. According to most biographical accounts of Morgan's life, safety officials informed the anxious relatives hovering near the tunnel opening that there was no way to reach the trapped men without further loss of life. The tunnel workers appeared doomed until someone at the waterworks remembered seeing a recent sales demonstration of Garrett Morgan's gas inhalator.

Messengers dashed off to contact Morgan and found him asleep at home. Informed of the crisis, he rushed to the tunnel with his brother Frank, aware that every second's delay was critical. At 2 A.M., the brothers and two volunteers donned Morgan smoke hoods and descended into the tunnel carrying several spare hoods. They located the site of the explosion and found the unconscious workers. After outfitting the victims in hoods, each dragged a worker back to the tunnel elevator and returned for another worker.

The Morgans and their helpers worked far into the night, making trip after trip into the poisonous tunnel. They carried thirty-two men to safety, men who would have died of asphyxiation had they not been so promptly rescued, as well as a number of dead. The publicity from this miraculous rescue unleashed a flood of orders for Morgan's invention. Morgan was besieged by requests to talk about and demonstrate his marvelous device in cities and towns all over the country.

News reports from those on the scene of the Cleveland Waterworks tunnel disaster, however, reported a story vastly different from the commonly accepted version.

By the time Morgan was summoned to the scene, nearly eleven hours had passed. According to the *New York Times,* "This afternoon a third rescue party, equipped with safety devices, entered the tunnel and recovered the rescuers, 10 of whom were dead." Protected by the Morgan helmet, the Morgan brothers and two volunteers descended into the lethal atmosphere of the tunnel. They hauled Van Duzen and a five other unconscious rescuers to the surface; only Van Duzen and one other person survived. The team also retrieved the bodies of those who died trying to reach the trapped tunnelers. Altogether, ten members of the two rescue parties died in a futile attempt to save the trapped tunnelers.

Mine experts accompanying the rescuers determined that the atmosphere was too explosive to risk any further effort at recovery until the gas could be pumped out. The tunnel was buried under so many tons of rock, mud, and debris that digging down to the trapped men, who were certainly dead, would take days. According to contemporary accounts, then, far from rescuing over thirty victims, Morgan saved two people. Presumably, his apparatus also saved the lives of those who descended in the third rescue party.

The apparent exaggeration of the incident was not necessary. Whether Morgan saved two or thirty, the tragedy clearly showed that his gas inhalator was effective and could have saved at least the lives of ten rescuers had it been available. Publicity from the incident triggered an increase in Morgan's sales. The city of Cleveland eventually recognized Morgan's work, awarding him a gold medal for his contributions to public safety.

Morgan's invention proved timely for American troops leaving to fight in the trenches of Europe in 1917. During World War I, armies tried to dislodge their entrenched enemies by aiming clouds of poisonous gas at them. American combat soldiers used an improved version of the Morgan hood as a gas mask to fight off the deadly clouds of chlorine gas sent at them by the enemy.

Morgan may have saved even more lives with an invention that he developed in the 1920s. While driving his automobile in Cleveland, Morgan witnessed a gruesome accident between a horse-drawn carriage and an automobile. As the drivers approached an intersection from different directions, each believed he could proceed safely; instead, they smashed into each other. Morgan saw passengers in the carriage fly through the air, and the driver of the car knocked unconscious. As more and more Americans purchased automobiles, such accidents were becoming increasingly common. The only way to direct traffic was to station a police officer at each intersection, an impractical solution.

Morgan developed a signpost that would regulate traffic coming from all four directions at an intersection. He devised an ingenious rotating traffic signal. The word "stop" was printed in large letters on the two opposite sides of two rectangles that faced the traffic to be stopped. The word "go" was printed on the end of the rectangle, which faced the traffic to proceed. When the rectangular blocks were at half-mast, this alerted everyone approaching the intersection to proceed with caution, because the signal was about to change. The signal could be electronically rotated at regular intervals to give each car a chance to move. Morgan's design also provided for all signs to go up at regular intervals to allow pedestrians to cross the intersection. Morgan proposed having the signs electrically lit so they would be visible at night as well as during the day.

Morgan received a patent for his traffic signal on November 20, 1923. By this time, he enjoyed a reputation as one of America's foremost inventors, and patent rights to his inventions commanded a high price. General Electric paid him the astounding sum of $40,000 for the rights to his traffic signal, the prototype on which current traffic lights are based.

Garrett Morgan took an active interest in his community and his fellow African Americans. He was involved in civil rights from his first days as a business operator helping to organize the Cleveland Association of Colored Men in 1908. In 1931, he ran for the city council with a promise of fair representation, equality, improved housing opportunities, and relief for the unemployed, but was not elected.

He enjoyed good health until stricken with glaucoma in his later years. Each year from 1943 to 1959 he traveled to the Mayo Clinic to receive the best treatment available for this eye disease, but his eyesight steadily worsened. Yet even when he was legally blind, Morgan persisted in his work, inventing an electric curling comb in 1960.

Morgan struggled with a number of illnesses in his final years. As he weakened, he told friends that he wanted to live long enough to attend the huge celebration in Chicago honoring the 100th anniversary of the Emancipation Proclamation. He missed his goal by one month, dying on July 27, 1963. It was one of the few goals this versatile inventor ever failed to achieve.

Chronology

MARCH 4, 1877	Garrett Augustus Morgan born in Claysville, Kentucky
1891	leaves home to find work in Cincinnati
1895	moves to Cleveland and begins work as a sewing machine adjuster for Roots and McBride
1907	opens his own sewing machine repair and sales shop
1908	marries Mary Ann Hasek
1909	expands business into tailoring clothes
1914	patents Morgan hood
1916	Great Cleveland Waterworks tunnel explosion
1923	patents electric traffic signal
1931	runs unsuccessfully for Cleveland city council
1943	begins treatment for glaucoma
1960	invents an electric curling iron
JULY 27, 1963	dies at age eighty-six

Further Reading

Brodie, James Michael, *Created Equal: The Lives and Ideas of Black American Innovators*. New York: William Morrow, 1993. A straightforward collective biography that includes an entry on Morgan.

Hayden, Robert C., *Nine African-American Inventors.* Frederick, Md.: Twenty-first Century Books, 1992. A collective biography that contains an exaggerated report of the Cleveland fire.

Jenkins, Edward, et al., *American Scientists and Inventors.* District of Columbia: National Science Teachers Association, 1975. This slim, unpretentious volume contains details about Morgan's pose as an Indian not found elsewhere.

Frederick Jones

(1892–1961)

Hungry and nearly destitute on the streets of Chicago, nineteen-year-old Frederick Jones decided to swallow his pride. On a September night in 1912, he boarded a train that would take him back to his hometown of Cincinnati, intending to humbly ask the owner of Crother's Garage to give him back the job he quit months before. Over the winter, perhaps he could make enough money to go to a farm in desperate need of mechanics he had heard about in Hallock, Minnesota.

When dawn arrived, Jones found himself in the town of Effingham, Illinois. He had taken the wrong train and was now more than 300 miles from Cincinnati. Desperate for food, Jones knocked on the back door of the Pacific House Hotel and asked if there was some work he could do in exchange for a meal. It happened that Charles Miller, who had just sold the hotel, was trying to get the old steam boiler furnace to work before turning the building over to the new owner.

Although Jones knew nothing about furnaces, he agreed to do the work. A man from the local hardware store answered his questions

Fred Jones (Courtesy of Thermo King)

and let him borrow the tools he needed. But Jones had to figure most of it out on his own. After more than a month's work, Jones nervously fired up the furnace, hoping he had done the job right.

He had. Jones later recalled, "I didn't know what would happen. I half expected that old boiler to blow up the hotel! But luck was with me . . . That job gave me a lot of confidence." Miller was so impressed with Jones's work that he asked him to join his family on a trip to their new farm in Minnesota. The Millers could use a skilled handyman to help them get their equipment going. Where was the farm? Jones asked. Near Hallock, came the answer.

Jones could hardly believe his roundabout good fortune. Riding with the livestock in a freight train, he traveled with the Millers to Hallock, where he began to carve out a new life as one of the most gifted inventors of the twentieth century. By the time he was through tinkering with equipment, his inventions would alter the American lifestyle and diet forever.

Frederick McKinley Jones was another African-American mechanical wizard raised in the Ohio Valley. He was born in Covington, Kentucky in 1892 to an Irish railroad worker and an African-American mother. Fred had no memories of his mother and believed she died when he was an infant. For the first nine years of his life, Fred moved from rooming house to rooming house with his father and spent much of the time alone while his father worked. He endured the taunts of others who made fun of his mixed-race heritage.

When Fred was seven, his father decided the boy needed more care than he could offer. The two walked across the bridge over the Ohio River to Cincinnati and looked up a priest named Father Ryan. Promising that he would come back for him some day, Fred's father left the boy with the priest and never returned.

Father Ryan enrolled Fred in school for the first time and imposed a strict discipline that was a far cry from the unstructured freedom he had enjoyed. Fred did as he was told for four years but then ran away at the age of twelve. Fascinated by automobiles ever since a neighboring chaffeur took him for ride, he sought work at R. C. Crothers's auto repair garage. Jones lied about his age and was told he could start out by sweeping the garage on Monday morning. At 6 A.M. on Saturday, mechanics found Jones camped on the garage doorstep, ready to work.

Jones watched and learned from the mechanics while sweeping and cleaning the shop. When he came up with questions that others could not answer, he went to the public library and checked out books to find the answers. He spent so much of his earnings on car magazines that he had to get a second job as a pin-setter in a bowling alley to support himself. By the time he was fourteen, Jones worked his way up to the position of mechanic; a year later, he was shop foreman.

Mr. Crothers loved to race automobiles, and often had a racing car in the shop to be worked on by his mechanics. Jones enjoyed the challenge of finding ways to pump power into a car engine. After designing and building a couple of racers for his employer from stripped down autos, Jones thought he deserved the chance to race one. Crothers not only refused to let him drive but ordered Jones to mind the garage while other employees went to the races.

On the day of a big race, Jones left the garage early and took a ferry to the racetrack, forty miles away. Upset that his mechanic had disobeyed orders, Mr. Crothers temporarily suspended Jones from his job. Rather than accept the punishment, Jones quit and headed south. Surely, he thought, a skilled mechanic would have no trouble finding work. But white employers just laughed at Jones's claim to be an accomplished mechanic, and he roamed throughout Kentucky, Tennessee, and Missouri, barely subsisting on odd jobs. After a brief spell working on a sightseeing steamboat in St. Louis, he moved to Chicago. There, the only job he found was a temporary position at a garage. While at the garage, he impressed one of his customers, a potato farmer from Hallock, Minnesota. The farmer advised Jones to move to Hallock, where Walter Hill, son of the wealthy railroad tycoon James J. Hill, was looking for a mechanic to work on a fleet of cars and equipment. Following his accidental trip to Effingham, in 1912 Jones stepped off a train in the northwest corner of Minnesota, far from towns of any size, in the middle of a Christmas Day blizzard.

After staying with the Millers for the winter, Jones walked several miles out to the Hill farm. Hill hired Jones on the spot. Jones felt like a kid in a candy shop as he worked on a fleet of farm equipment that included steam engines, milk machines, tractors, graders, harvesters, and automobiles. When he was not working on machines, he thought about them. Jones spent many nights reading books on engines and electronics, trying to learn from others what he could not figure out for himself.

Jones made many friends in Hallock who showed him the pleasures of rural life, such as fishing and hunting in the woods. "Casey" Jones, as his friends nicknamed him, also found people with whom he could share his musical interests. He not only sang in a quartet but played saxophone in a town band.

The fun lasted until Walter Hill's father died in 1916. Walter sold the farm and moved to St. Paul, leaving Jones without a job. After working through the fall on a threshing crew in North Dakota, Jones returned to Hallock and got a job as a mechanic in Oscar Younggren's garage. Younggren was another auto shop owner with an interest in auto racing. He gave Jones the green light to juice up old cars using whatever scraps and used-car parts he could find, and permission to race the cars. Jones rebuilt and modified a Dodge into a racing vehicle called "Number 15," which became a crowd favorite at county fair dirt track races.

When the United States called for volunteers to fight in World War I, Jones enlisted in the 809th Pioneer Infantry. He disliked the segregation of the armed forces that assigned him to an all-black unit, but he served in France and proved valuable as an electrician, mechanic, and all-around handyman.

Jones returned to Hallock in 1919 and took "Number 15" back on the race circuit. Although he drew cheers from fans and frequently won prize money, Jones continued to battle prejudice. Hotels often refused to let rooms to blacks. At a race in South Dakota, the other nineteen drivers secretly agreed to block Jones at every opportunity to make sure he did not win the race. The strategy backfired, however: Jones won the race while five cars were smashed trying to box him.

By the mid-1920s, Jones and other mechanics were producing souped-up engines too powerful to control on the tightly curved tracks. In 1925, Jones accepted an invitation to compete at some international races in Chicago. Jones sat at a racetrack watching other races, biding time before his five-mile event later in the day. As he looked on in horror, several cars crashed spectacularly, causing three deaths. Jones had to walk through a pool of blood to get to his car for his race.

Sickened by the experience, Jones nervously started his engine. During the race he nearly suffered the same fate. He lost control in the middle of a turn, and spun sideways into a fence. "Number 15" crashed through several posts before finally coming to a stop. Jones flew out of the car and was knocked unconscious. Although he recovered fully from his injuries, Jones never regained his passion for racing.

Jones turned his attention from automotives to electronics, and soon introduced Hallock to many new devices, including some of his own remarkable inventions. Self-taught from books and tinkering, Jones constructed a transmitter for a new radio station in Hallock and built radios for customers. He invented what was probably the world's first portable X-ray machine for the local hospital, but since he did it for a friend it never occurred to him to patent it.

When Duffy and Geneva Larson took over management of the Grand Theater in 1927, they had a rude surprise. The motion picture industry had begun to produce sound records to go with the movies, which previously had been silent films with subtitles. Unfortunately, the cost for this new sound equipment was far more than the new owners could afford. Since Hollywood was phasing out silent films, it looked as though the theater would have to shut down. But, like many Hallock residents with a technical problem, the Larsons approached "Casey" Jones. As usual, he came through with a home-made creation that was as good as or better than the state-of-the-art equipment. Using leather machine belts and parts he stripped from junked automobiles and plows, and a few purchased components, he put together a sound unit for less than 100 dollars. The device was so complex that Fred had to be present to start every movie.

A few years later, the movie industry discovered a way to record the sound directly onto the film. Again, this required new motion picture projector equipment that the Larsons could not afford. Jones obtained books describing how the system worked, then set to work building his own unit. He ground glass from a towel rod over his sink into a tiny lens, then connected the rod to a photoelectric cell. The device produced a narrow beam of light that Jones aimed at the film; when the beam hit the moving film it activated the sound.

Word of the incredible sound system Jones produced in his own shop on a shoestring budget spread across the state to Minneapolis. Joseph Numero, whose Ultraphone Sound Systems company sold theater equipment, was under siege from theater owners frustrated by problems with the standard sound equipment. Numero heard about Jones and sent a letter to Duffy Larson, recruiting Jones to come to Minneapolis to work for him as a technical expert. Despite his misgivings about leaving Hallock for the big city, Jones arrived in Numero's office. Upon seeing he was black, Numero immediately dismissed him, until Jones convinced him that he was the Hallock electronics wizard.

Used to being his own boss, Jones ignored the expected working hours and company policies and was frequently absent from the job. Other supervisors resented this, but Numero, recognizing Jones's

> "When I walked into [Numero's] shop, I never wanted to leave. I felt the same way I did when I walked into the Crothers' Garage when I was twelve years old. Here in one place was everything I needed to try out the ideas going 'round my head."
>
> —Frederick Jones

special talent, let him operate his own way. Numero's patience paid immediate dividends. While working as an engineer for Ultraphone, Jones develope a superior sound system and his first patented invention—a machine for automatically dispensing tickets at the box-office window.

In 1937, a brutal heat wave settled on Minneapolis. One night Jones could no longer stand the heat in his home and went for a drive around one of the city's lakes. He rolled down the windows on the car and enjoyed a heavenly cool breeze from the lake. Unfortunately, the mosquitoes were out in droves that evening. Before long, the whining insects made Jones so miserable that he had to shut the windows. With the breeze shut off, the car became even hotter than his home. Jones returned home, grumbling that someone ought to invent a device that could air-condition a car.

The more Jones thought about it, the more the idea intrigued him. He did not know much about air-conditioning, but he knew where to go for information. The next morning, Jones headed to the Minneapolis public library to look up whatever he could find on air-conditioning and refrigeration. As far as he could tell from the sources he found, no one had ever built a successful car air conditioner.

He spent his spare time that week putting together plans and sketching designs for such a device. Excited by the possibilities, he presented his idea to his boss. Numero glanced at a sketch and shook his head. Air conditioners were too big and heavy to fit into a car, and far too expensive. At any rate, Numero made his living selling theater equipment and was not interested in exploring an entirely new type of business. While Jones he did not pursue the idea any further with Numero, he continued to research the subject of air conditioners; perhaps he could develop one the company could sell to cool theaters.

On an unusually hot afternoon in May 1938, some high-powered Minneapolis business executives met for a game of golf. Joe Numero of Ultraphone Sound Systems teed off with Max Winter, who later owned the Minnesota Vikings, Al Fineberg, president of an air-conditioning company, and Harry Werner, owner of the Werner Transportation Company.

While the foursome was out on the course, Werner received an urgent phone call. He returned to his golf mates, fuming. One of his trucks had broken down en route to Chicago and its entire shipment of chickens spoiled in the hot sun. That wasn't the first time Werner had lost a valuable shipment to spoilage. Werner took out his frustration on Fineberg, demanding to know why his company couldn't manufacture an air conditioner for trucks. Fineberg

Jones working on a cooling system improvement for Thermo King (Courtesy of Thermo King)

explained the difficulty. First, the delicate mechanism of an air conditioner could not withstand the bumping and jarring of a truck over the road. Even if it could, where would a moving truck get the large amount of electricity needed to run it?

Numero couldn't resist needling Fineberg. He told Werner that if Fineberg wouldn't build him an air-conditioned trailer, Numero would be happy to do the job. "I suppose your man Jones could make a machine for Harry's trailer," scoffed Fineberg. Still joking, Numero bragged that Jones could do it with no problem. At the time, he forgot that Jones once asked about the possibility of air-conditioned vehicles. A few days later, Werner called Numero to tell him that he had bought a new twenty-four-foot trailer truck and was sending it to Numero's shop to have the cooling unit installed. Numero could not believe what he was hearing; he hadn't imagined that Werner would take him seriously.

Once again, Fred Jones came to the rescue. He went out to Werner's truck and began taking measurements. After about half an hour, he informed Numero that he could do the job. Using shock-proofing techniques he developed when building racers, Jones put together a 2,200-pound cooling unit powered by a four-cylinder gas engine. Although the unit worked, Jones thought it was "clunky" and inefficient. He redesigned the cooling unit to trim 400 pounds from its weight.

Jones's invention worked so well that Numero applied for a patent and decided to switch to an entirely new line of products. He sold Ultraphone and all of Jones's innovations to RCA and formed a new company called U.S. Thermo Control to manufacture and sell small, shock-proof automated cold-storage equipment for trucks.

While Numero was pleased with Jones's invention, the perfectionist Jones thought it did not run as efficiently as it should. He studied every aspect of his cooling unit and discovered the problem lay in the placement of the unit under the trailer. Sand, mud, and flying gravel from the road clogged the unit until it could barely function.

Jones redesigned his air conditioner, splitting it into two parts. The gas engine, compressor, and condenser were all mounted high on the outside of the trailer; the rest of the unit went inside the trailer. Together, both parts of Jones's invention weighed less than 1,000 pounds, yet was constructed so solidly that it could withstand road shock and vibration. It was this design that transformed the fledgling U.S. Thermo Control company into the multimillion dollar Thermo King Corporation that radically changed America's eating habits by its ability to bring refrigerated products safely to the market.

Despite his success, Jones kept experimenting with ways to improve his refrigeration units. He discovered that food products could go bad very quickly, even in an air-conditioned compartment, if the temperature could not be kept constant throughout the compartment, or if the humidity was too high or low. Jones found ways to regulate moisture content and keep air circulating evenly throughout the compartment. Jones even added a reverse cycle mechanism for producing heat to prevent cargo from freezing when trucks traveled in bitterly cold temperatures.

Jones patented a total of sixty-one inventions, forty of them affecting mobile refrigeration equipment. Many of his ideas were soon adapted for use in railroad cars, cargo ships, and airplanes. Fred reportedly rode a quarter of a million miles in railroad cars, testing his products.

Jones's inventions provided a huge boost to transportation industries and farmers by opening new long-distance markets for their products. Prior to the refrigerated trucks Jones introduced, oranges were a rare and expensive holiday treat in northern climates. The only meat for sale was whatever the local butcher had on hand, and the milk was available only from a local dairy. The only fresh fruits and vegetables, dairy products, and meats for a reasonable price on the market were those produced locally. Frozen foods could be delivered to stores only a limited distance from the factory. Thanks to Jones's inventions, food is routinely shipped in from hundreds and even thousands of miles away. The number of food products available to the average consumer is limited solely by the imagination of the producers. The availability of small, efficient, automated refrigeration units for food carriers changed the eating habits of the entire nation, particularly by helping the distribution of newly improved frozen food products.

Jones also save lives with his cold storage innovations. During World War II, he designed the portable air-conditioning unit used

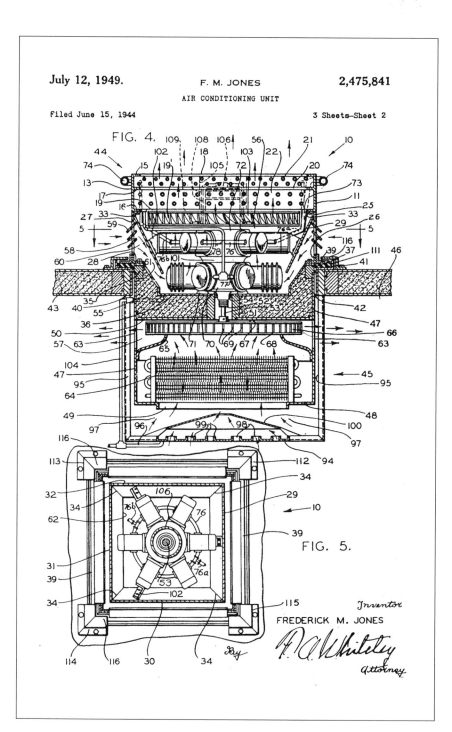

Patent diagram of Jones's revolutionary truck air-conditioning unit (U.S. Patent Office)

at military field hospitals. This allowed the military to store perishable, life-saving medicines and blood serum close to the battlefield, even in the sweltering islands of the Pacific Ocean.

Impressed by his engineering expertise, the United States Department of Defense and the Bureau of Standards hired Jones as a consultant in the later years of his career. Jones continued to live in Minneapolis with his wife, Lucille, whom he married in 1946, and work for Thermo King. Since by agreement his company owned his patents, Jones never made a great deal of money from his inventions. That didn't seem to bother him, nor did the fact that during their long relationship, Numero never invited Jones to his home. Although other companies offered him far more money than he was making at Thermo King, he refused to consider moving. "Leave Thermo King and my babies to take another job?" he exclaimed. "Just for money?" Frederick McKinley Jones died, still virtually unknown to most of the country, in Minneapolis on February 21, 1961.

Chronology

1892	Frederick McKinley Jones born in Covington, Kentucky
1899	Dad leaves him with Father Ryan in Cincinnati
1904	runs away, finds work at R. C. Crothers's garage
1909	suspended from job, quits and travels looking for work
SEPTEMBER 1912	accidently arrives in Effingham, Illinois; fixes a motel furnace
DECEMBER 1912	arrives in Hallock, Minnesota
1913	begins working at Walter Hill's estate

1916	moves to town, joins Oscar Younggren's garage
1918	enlists in the U.S. Army in World War I
1919	returns to Hallock, continues racing and handyman work
1925	quits racing after multiple auto race tragedies in Chicago
1927	creates sound system for Grand Theater in Hallock
CA. 1930	moves to Minneapolis; begins work for Joseph Numero at Ultraphone
1938	begins work on refrigerated truck
1939	receives first patent, for ticket-dispensing machine; markets first refrigerated unit for trucks
1946	marries Lucille Powell
1948	begins testing refrigeration unit for trains
FEBRUARY 21, 1961	dies at age sixty-eight

Further Reading

Swanson, Gloria M., and Margaret V. Ott, *I've Got an Idea!: The Story of Frederick McKinley Jones.* Minneapolis: Runestone Press, 1994. This book is the most detailed and complete account of Jones's life.

Percy Julian

(1899–1975)

Percy Julian and his assistant Josef Pikl were working most of the night in their DePauw University laboratory, setting up an experiment that could change their lives. If all went according to plan, the chemists could celebrate a breakthrough they had been pursuing for nearly five years: the synthesis of physostigmine—a muscle relaxant used in the treatment of glaucoma. Glaucoma, which received national attention in 1996 when it sidelined baseball star Kirby Puckett, is an eye disease that destroys the retina and eventually causes blindness.

Sometime after midnight, the two scientists heated two small test tubes. Pikl's tube contained crystals of natural physostigmine obtained from Calabar beans. Julian's tube held crystals of a synthetically formed chemical that the researchers *hoped* was physostigmine. If the crystals in the two tubes started melting at exactly the same temperature, the scientists would have proof that they had synthesized the substance.

Percy Julian (Schomburg Center for Research in Black Culture)

Julian stared at the crystals and the thermometer as the temperature in the test tube rose. Suddenly, the crystal dissolved into a liquid "It's melting!" Pikl cried. "Mine too!" Julian answered. The two fell into each other's arms in jubilant celebration. The exhausting effort had been worth it.

We often think of inventors as mechanical wonders who, with their own hands and some basic workshop tools, build a useful gadget. But a great deal of inventing in the twentieth century takes place not in the shop but in the laboratory, not with handyman's tools but with test tubes. These inventors do not create gadgets or machines, but rather combine chemicals and tinker with genes to construct new medicines, materials, and even life-forms.

For most of American history, few African Americans had access to the higher education required to pioneer exciting new developments in the pure sciences. Percy Julian blazed a trail through a hostile scientific and academic community to patent more than 100 chemical inventions.

Percy Levon Julian was born on April 11, 1899, in Montgomery, Alabama, the eldest of six children born to James and Elizabeth Julian. The family considered education a sacred privilege. No one could forget the severe price one of Percy's grandfathers had paid for knowledge: a slave owner chopped off two of the man's fingers after discovering him secretly trying to learn to read and write.

Percy's grandmother Lavonia, an ex-slave who was something of a legend for once picking 350 pounds of cotton in a single day, took pride in sending her children to school. One of the teachers, Joan Stuart, told her that her son James had exceptional ability. Stuart spoke highly of a college, DePauw University, that was near her home town in Indiana.

From that moment, Lavonia was determined to give James the opportunity to make the most of his talent. Rather than spending the earnings from her small produce farm on herself, she saved to send James to a private black high school. Lavonia continued to save in the hope of sending James to DePauw, but he was never able to go. Instead of giving up on his dream, James transferred it to his children.

James Julian made sure his children took their education seriously. Once Percy received a score of 80 percent on a school paper, one of the highest grades in the class, and came home from school proudly bearing the proof of his achievement. Instead of complimenting him, James sat his son down and lectured him about working up to his ability: he did not expect to be satisfied with anything less than 100 percent. Elizabeth Percy, who taught school, was more encouraging, but equally determined to give her children the best education possible.

The Julians sent Percy to the same private blacks-only school that his father had attended. Percy once sneaked over to the white school to peek in the windows. He looked at the laboratory facilities and other equipment that his school did not have and wished that some day he would get a chance to work in a similar laboratory.

Facilities were so lacking at Percy's school that he transferred to the Normal School for Negroes, one of the few high schools for blacks in the South. Julian performed so well that upon his graduation in 1916, he earned a college scholarship. His ninety-nine-year-old grandmother, tears of joy streaming down her face, waved goodbye as the lad traveled to Greencastle, Indiana to attend what had for so long been the Julian family's promised land—DePauw University.

This rewarding experience began as a nightmare. Julian, the proud honors student, suffered the humiliation of being classified as a "subfreshman." Julian's previous schools, although the best available in his area for blacks, had operated on such meager funds that Julian was in many areas far behind the average freshman. He had to take a number of high school classes as well as a full college load during his first two years at DePauw to rise to college standards.

As the only black on campus, Julian felt isolated. He slept in the attic of a fraternity house where he worked as a waiter to help pay for his schooling. His love of music was useful, and he made extra money playing with a jazz band at dances. Occasionally, he would find refuge by staying with a local black family for a weekend, or by spending a night at the Indianapolis YMCA.

Julian worked hard and not only caught up to his classmates but shot past them. Majoring in chemistry, Julian graduated at the top of his 160-member class in 1920. His parents were so impressed by what he accomplished at DePauw that most of his family moved to Greencastle, and his brothers and sisters followed him to DePauw. Eventually, his two brothers earned doctorates and his sisters all achieved master's degrees. During this time, Percy's father remained behind in Montgomery so that he could support the family from his earnings as a railroad mail clerk.

"There went my dreams and hopes of four years. As I pressed my lips to hold back the tears, I remembered my breeding, braced myself, and thanked [Blanchard] for thinking of me."

—Percy Julian

Having succeeded spectacularly, Julian now prepared to reap the reward of his hard work. Colleges customarily recommend their best students for scholarships at top graduate schools, and then inform them when they are accepted. Julian eagerly awaited word of where he would be spending the next few years. But as one after another of DePauw's chemistry students got word of acceptance to a graduate school, Julian heard nothing. He continued to wait, hoping that the schools were saving the best for last. Finally, he could stand the suspense no longer. He met with Dr. W. M. Blanchard, the chair of DePauw's chemistry department. Blanchard broke the sad news that no graduate school wanted Julian. Everyone agreed that Julian would be wasting his time because he would never be able to make use of a graduate education. No business would hire a black chemist for an advanced position, nor would any major university or college hire him. The best Julian could hope for in his chosen field was to teach at a Negro college, and for that he did not need any advanced degrees.

Julian was stunned by the news. Reluctantly, he accepted the only choice available to him. He joined the faculty of Fisk University, an exclusively black college in Nashville, Tennessee. There, he gave lectures that, according to Blanchard, "are so clear, I'm going to tear up many of my own and use yours instead." Julian discovered, to his pleasant surprise, that the experts were wrong about the quality of students, who were constantly challenging him to the limits of his knowledge. Julian decided he had to have more education in his field.

Encouraged by a report that a black student broke through the academic barriers in the United States and received a Ph.D. in chemistry, Julian discarded the warnings about wasting his time at graduate school; he obtained a fellowship to attend a graduate school program at Harvard University. Although he performed brilliantly at Harvard and earned his master's degree in 1922, administrators refused to grant him a position as a teaching assistant in fear that white students would take offense at having a black instructor.

In 1926, Julian accepted a position at West Virginia State College, another all-black school. There he struggled for a year with virtually no laboratory as the school's only chemistry professor. Frustrated at the lack of facilities for research, Julian moved on to yet another all-black college, Howard University in Washington, D.C. While at Howard, Julian planned and supervised the construction of a million-dollar laboratory and received a grant allowing him to travel to Vienna, Austria to study for his Ph.D. in organic chemistry. His mentor, Ernst Spath, was an expert in the synthesis of chemicals.

Julian learned that European scientists were interested in soybeans as a source of many valuable chemicals difficult to produce by artificial means. Among these chemicals was physostigmine. No one knew exactly how physostigmine worked, much less how to synthesize it in a laboratory. Working with Josef Pikl, Julian combed through all the reports he could find on the substance. He broke down physostigmine into simpler organic compounds and then looked for these compounds in plants and animals. Julian traced the natural processes by which these compounds were changed into physostigmine.

The project proved to be an enormous undertaking. The process of breaking physostigmine down into simpler units and determining how to reconstruct those units was painfully slow. Many of his colleagues doubted that Julian was on the right track because some of his research on natural chemical synthesis contradicted the findings of the world's leading expert on the subject, Dr. Robert Robinson of Oxford University, England.

Undaunted, Julian continued his work and returned to Howard University after receiving his Ph.D., which he wrote in German, in 1931. As he and his assistants continued their steady progress, Julian fell into a disagreement with Howard University administrators and began looking for other employment.

This time Dr. Blanchard was able to give the assistance that he had been unable to offer at Julian's graduation. Hearing that Julian was out of work, Dr. Blanchard arranged to have him appointed to the staff of the chemistry department at DePauw and found funds for him to continue his physostigmine research. In 1934, working at DePauw, Julian announced that he and Pikl identified all the basic components and the structure of the substance.

Yet again the elusive prize seemed likely to slip from his grasp. Even as worldwide praise was showered on Julian for his research, DePauw yielded to financial pressures and withdrew its support of Julian's work. This time the nonprofit Rosenwald Foundation came to the rescue, offering to finance Julian's entire research effort for two years. Within a year, Julian synthesized physostigmine, and shortly thereafter set up a workable process for synthesizing the compound.

Julian made 1935 a truly memorable year by marrying Dr. Anna Johnson, a sociologist at MacMurray College in Illinois. Yet the rewards of his efforts were slow in coming. Dr. Blanchard tried to promote Julian to the chair of the chemistry department at DePauw, but others blocked the move. Julian continued to run into locked doors at the academic institutions where he hoped to teach. No one outside of the traditionally all-black colleges expressed an interest in a black professor. The Institute of Paper Chemists in Appleton, Wisconsin, came forward to offer Julian a research position. But when the administrators discovered that Appleton had an ordinance prohibiting the overnight housing of blacks, they had to withdraw the offer.

The Glidden Company, which dealt in chemical-based products, decided that Julian's experience with soybean chemistry was too valuable to ignore. In 1936, Julian accepted a job as director of research of Glidden's Soy Products Division. The chemist who had been forced to hop from place to place finally settled into the business world.

When Julian took over the soybean program at Glidden, his new employers asked what he thought of their program to date. Julian summed up the situation in three words: "Gentlemen, it's lousy," he said. The aroma from the proteins the team was isolating smelled so bad, Julian could not keep his lunch down while working with them. Julian was able to eliminate a bacteria that produced the terrible stench.

Julian then worked on isolating and synthesizing sterols from soybeans. His first product was a protein to be used in place of the milk protein casein in the process of coating paper so that ink would adhere better and for waterproofing cardboard cartons. Julian could produce his soy protein at a fraction of the cost of casein.

The chemist's most dramatic innovation was the development of a soy protein for use as a fire extinguisher. Julian's concoction, affectionately known as "bean soup" aboard U. S. Navy ships, could douse oil and gas fires not extinguishable by water. This material saved countless sailors from painful deaths during World War II.

Prior to Julian's work, substances derived from sterols were so expensive that few patients could afford their use. Sterols are the basic chemical building blocks of hormones, which regulate a number of body functions. Almost all commercial sterols came from European companies, which extracted them from the bile of animal livers, primarily ox livers. Lab technicians had to process many tons of ox livers to squeeze out just a small amount of sterol; over 15,000 ox livers were required for enough sterol to treat one patient for one year.

Soybean oil contained ample supplies of sterols, but during the extraction process it hardened into an impenetrable mass. As every attempt to dissolve the sterols from this mass failed, Julian grew discouraged. One day, he watched a friend who was at work making a substance to prevent plaster from setting too quickly. When the friend added quicklime, the substance boiled and fizzed into a porous form. Julian decided to add quicklime to soybean oil. The quicklime changed the oil into a foam from which the sterols could be more easily extracted.

Julian at work in laboratory facilities beyond his wildest dreams as a young student
(Schomburg Center for Research in Black Culture)

PERCY JULIAN

Julian's synthetic production slashed the cost of sterols from several hundred dollars per gram to about 20 cents per gram. This made it possible for hundreds of thousands of patients to initiate treatment with cortisone, a hormone that reduced swelling in tissues and joints. Cortisone was used initially to treat a painful condition known as arthritis. Since discontinued as an arthritis treatment because of harmful side effects, cortisone and other sterols continue to be used for a variety of medical purposes, including the treatment of inflamed joints.

After nearly two decades at Glidden, Julian went off on his own. In 1953, he founded the Julian Institute in Franklin Park, Illinois, for the purpose of producing products, particularly sex hormones from sterols. To take advantage of the discovery that a type of wild yam growing in Mexico produced large amounts of hormones, Julian built a new facility, Laboratorios de México, in Mexico City. His business was a great success, generating a profit of nearly $100,000 in its second year.

While Julian was crashing with ease through scientific barriers, social barriers were another matter. Shortly after his success in synthesizing cortisone, he and Anna bought a house in Oak Park, a prosperous Chicago suburb that billed itself "the middle class capital of the world." The water commissioner refused to turn on the water to the house. While the house was being decorated before the Julians moved in, two men broke into the house and poured gasoline in all the rooms. They tossed a torch in through a window and raced off in a car. Fortunately, the torch did not immediately ignite the fuel, and an alert neighbor summoned the fire department before any real damage was done. The Julians hired security guards and a bulldog to watch the house twenty-four hours a day.

Nonetheless, during their first year in the neighborhood, bigots struck again. While Percy and Anna traveled to Baltimore to attend a funeral, vandals in a speeding car tossed a bomb into their house. The Julian's two children, seven-year-old Faith and eleven-year-old Percy, were in the house, but escaped injury.

"We've lived through these things all our lives. As far as the hurt to the spirit goes, we've been accustomed to that."

—Percy Julian

Julian refused to let a bunch of hateful people bully his family out of their home. Knowing firsthand the value of education, he insisted on staying in the neighborhood of his choice, where his children could benefit from a good school system. He saw no reason why blacks should be squeezed into inner city ghettos "as nourishing as a desert," from which only the exceptionally gifted and fortunate could escape.

Julian battled prejudice in his profession through most of his life. Once he was invited to attend a meeting of a national science society only to have the invitation withdrawn because the meeting was being held at a club that refused to admit African Americans. Julian was equally irritated by reverse prejudice, especially when he thought society was giving him special treatment to make up for past racial wrongs. After being named "Chicagoan of the Year" by the Chicago Sun Times and Junior Chamber of Commerce, Julian questioned the honor. In his acceptance speech he said, "I appreciate deeply all this outpouring of good will, but I don't know why you should so honor me, except I belong to a race which hangs heavily on your conscience." Julian was being modest; he fashioned a career worthy of the highest honors. When DePauw University named a chemistry and mathematics building after him, it did so because he ranked among the top scientists America has produced.

Unlike most African-American inventors in U.S. history, Julian was able to convert his ideas to wealth. In the early 1960s, he sold his company to the Chicago pharmaceutical firm of Smith, Klein, and French for more than 2 million dollars. This enabled him to live comfortably through his retirement until his death from liver cancer on April 19, 1975.

Chronology

APRIL 11, 1899	Percy Levon Julian born in Montgomery, Alabama
1916	graduates from high school and earns a scholarship to DePauw University

1920	graduates first in his class from DePauw, yet cannot attract a single post-graduate offer. Accepts teaching position at Fisk University
1922	enters master's program at Harvard University
1926	teaches at West Virginia State College
1927	teaches at Howard University
1929	goes to Austria to study for his doctorate; begins working on physostigmine
1931	completes Ph.D.
1935	completes synthesis of physostigmine; marries Dr. Anna Johnson
1936	accepts position with Glidden as director of research for the Soy Products Division
1953	establishes the Julian Institute; moves to Oak Park, Chicago
1954	patents process for synthesizing cortisone
APRIL 19, 1975	dies at the age of seventy-six

Further Reading

Haber, Louis. *Black Pioneers of Science and Inventions.* New York: Harcourt, Brace and World, 1970. A young adult book with a chapter on Julian.

Yount, Lisa. *Black Scientists.* New York: Facts On File, 1991. Profiles eight black scientists, including Julian.

Index

Boldface page numbers indicate main topics. *Italic* page numbers indicate illustrations or captions.

INDEX